Kabbalah
&
Jewish
Mysticism

Rabbi Dan Cohn-Sherbok is Professor of Judaism at the
University of Wales, Lampeter. He is the author of over fifty books
on Jewish history and beliefs.

'Rabbi Cohn Sherbok deserves applause for the clarity and brevity
of this slim, engrossing introduction to Jewish mysticism.'
Publishers Weekly

'A concise and readable anthology of Jewish mystical documents
arranged in a clear chronological order.' *Library Journal*

D1118013

Dan Cohn-Sherbok

Kabbalah

&
Jewish
Mysticism

An Introductory Anthology

ONEWORLD
OXFORD

KABBALAH AND JEWISH MYSTICISM: AN INTRODUCTORY ANTHOLOGY

Oneworld Publications Limited
(Sales and Editorial)
185 Banbury Road
Oxford OX2 7AR
England

Oneworld Publications
(US Marketing Office)
www.oneworld-publications.com

© Dan Cohn-Sherbok 1995,2006

First edition 1995
Second edition 2006

ISBN-13-978-1-85168-454-0
ISBN-10:1-85168-454-9

Cover design by Design Deluxe
Typeset by SNP Best-set Typesetter Ltd., Hong Kong
Printed and bound by WS Bookwell, Finland

Contents

Preface

In recent years there has been an increasing interest in the Jewish mystical tradition, particularly given the attraction of kabbalah for Hollywood celebrities. Traditionally, the term 'kabbalah' refers to the teachings of Jewish mystics; it encompasses all the mystical teachings of Judaism, especially those that evolved from the time of the second Temple through the Middle Ages. The purpose of this volume is to provide a short account of the history of Jewish mysticism through the ages. Beginning with an introduction to the major developments of mystical reflection, the book continues with an anthology of mystical texts arranged chronologically. All anthologies are by nature selective – this collection is no different. Throughout I have sought to provide relatively short examples of some of the most important mystical sources from ancient times to the present. These various passages should ideally be read in connection with the introductory material, which provides a historical context for the emergence of mystical speculation.

Those who wish to delve deeper into this subject are encouraged to consult the various works listed below from which I have obtained information and source material: J. Abelson, *Jewish Mysticism* (Brooklyn, NY: Sepher-Hermon Press, 1969); David Ariel, *The Mystic Quest: An Introduction to Jewish Mysticism* (New York: Pantheon Books, 1992); David R. Blumenthal, *Understanding Jewish Mysticism: A Source Reader*, vols 1 and 2 (New York: Ktav Publishing House, 1978, 1982); Ben Zion Bokser, *The Jewish Mystical Tradition* (Northvale, NJ: Jason Aronson, 1983); Arthur Green (ed.) *Jewish Spirituality*, vols 1 and 2 (New York: Crossroad, 1986, 1987); Louis Jacobs, *Jewish Mystical Testimonies* (New York: Schocken Books, 1977); Aryeh Kaplan, *Meditation and Kabbalah* (Northvale, NJ:

Jason Aronson, 1995); Gershom Scholem, *Major Trends of Jewish Mysticism* (New York: Schocken Books, 1995); Gershom Scholem, *Zohar* (New York: Schocken Books, 1995); Robert Seltzer, *Jewish People, Jewish Thought* (New York: Macmillan, 1982); Isaiah Tishby, *The Wisdom of the Zohar*, vols 1 to 3, (Oxford: Oxford University Press, 1991).

Chronological Table

Patriarchal period	*c.*1900–*c.*1600 BCE
Exodus from Egypt	*c.*1250–*c.*1230 BCE
Period of the Judges	*c.*1200–*c.*1000 BCE
Period of the United Monarchy	*c.*1030–*c.*930 BCE
Division of the Kingdom	*c.*930 BCE
Elijah	ninth century BCE
Isaiah	eighth century BCE
Destruction of the Northern Kingdom (Israel) by the Assyrians	722 BCE
Destruction of the Southern Kingdom (Judah) by the Babylonians	586 BCE
Ezekiel	sixth century BCE
Babylonian Exile	586–538 BCE
Return of the Exiles	538 BCE
Rebuilding of the Temple in Jerusalem	*c.*520–*c.*515 BCE
Second Temple period	*c.*515 BCE–*c.*CE 70
Ezra and Nehemiah's reforms	*c.*450–*c.*400 BCE
Daniel	*c.*fifth century BCE
End of the period of prophecy	*c.*450 BCE
Torah given scriptural status	*c.*450 BCE
Hellenistic period	333–63 BCE
Prophets given scriptural status	*c.*200 BCE
Maccabean rebellion and Hasmonean period	167–163 BCE
Hasmonean revolt	166–164 BCE
Roman period	*c.*146 BCE–*c.*CE 400
Philo of Alexandria	first century BCE
New Testament written	*c.*50–90
Jewish rebellion against Rome	66–70

Modern period	c.1700–present
Moses Hayyim Luzzatto	1707–46
Baal Shem Tov	1700–60
Mystics of Bet El	c.eighteenth century
Vilna Gaon	1720–97
Hayyim of Volozhin	1749–1821
Alexander Susskind	eighteenth century
Nahman of Bratslav	1772–1811
Levi Yitzhak of Berdichev	c.1740–1810
Kalonymus Kalman Epstein	nineteenth century
Dov Baer of Mezhirich	c.1710–72
Shneur Zalman of Liady	1747–1813
Dov Baer of Lubavich	nineteenth century
Isaac Judah Jahiel Safrin	1806–74
Reform movement founded	c.1850
Conservative movement founded	c.1895
First Zionist Congress	1897
Aaron Roth	1894–1944
Modern Orthodoxy founded	c.1905
Abraham Isaac Kook	1865–1935
Reconstructionist movement founded	c.1935
Holocaust	1942–5
Founding of the State of Israel	1948

An Introduction to Jewish Mysticism

What is mysticism? The word itself appears to have originated from the mysteries of Ancient Greece. In all likelihood it was derived from the word *muein*, which means to close the lips or eyes – initiates to these secret cults were instructed to keep silent about what they experienced. Initially the Greek mysteries were associated with the Earth Mother and Dionysus, the god of vegetation and wine. Although these ceremonies are not known in detail, it appears that they involved purification by bathing in the sea, initiation, admission into advanced stages, a communion meal and a sacred marriage. Mysticism is thus rooted in the mysterious practices of the ancient world, yet from a religious perspective this term has undergone a fundamental shift in meaning.

In the world's religions the central aim of mysticism is to attain an apprehension of and union with the Divine. Within Judaism, the mystic is understood as one who seeks to gain an experience of God – this can be attained either through personal experience or intense speculation. In the history of the faith, mysticism has undergone a complex evolution beginning from the direct experience of the Patriarchs, Moses and the prophets, to the recondite cosmological and theological explanations of later rabbis. Yet, despite their differences in approach, Jewish sages have been united in their conviction that the spiritual quest is of paramount importance. The purpose of the religious life, they maintain, is to know God and experience His divine presence.

The Origins of Jewish Mysticism

The Hebrew Scriptures contain some of the most vivid and arresting depictions of divine encounter. Beginning with the Patriarchs –

Abraham, Isaac and Jacob – God is depicted as guiding the destiny of the Jewish nation. In Genesis, for example, God told Abraham to go to Canaan, where he and his descendants were to become a great multitude. Later God tested Abraham's dedication by ordering him to sacrifice his only son – it was only at the last moment that the Lord appeared to Abraham in the form of a divine messenger to tell him to desist. Subsequently God revealed himself to Jacob in a dream of majestic grandeur, promising that his descendants would inherit the land. In another passage, God disclosed himself to Jacob as a divine messenger, and in the gorge of the river Jabbok God wrestled with Jacob, bestowing upon him his new name Israel, which later denoted both the Jewish nation and the Promised Land.

After the ancient Israelites were enslaved in Egypt, God disclosed himself to Moses, calling him to free the Jewish people from bondage. Here again Scripture presents God's revelation in mysterious terms: out of a burning bush God commanded obedience to his will. On Mount Sinai God's theophany overwhelmed the nation – in fear and trembling they listened to the divine decree. In the prophetic books this tradition of divine revelation continued: from Elijah onwards the prophets spoke in God's name. Through direct communications, visions and dreams, the Lord disclosed himself to his faithful servants, demanding they rebuke the nation and foretell impending doom. Although these individuals were often overwhelmed by this encounter, they nonetheless were able to transform these experiences into public utterances about the fate of the nation and the final 'Day of the Lord'. The Bible thus serves as the basis of mystical experience in the life of the Jewish nation. It is here that God met his people, and this record of divine encounter serves as the background to the evolution of Jewish mystical reflection.

According to tradition, prophecy culminated during the period of the Second Temple. In the place of charismatic figures claiming to have had a direct experience of God, Jewish writers engaged in speculation about the nature of God and his relation to the world. Initially such theorizing was contained in biblical books as well as in non-canonical literature. Later, Hellenistic Jewish thinkers such as Philo of Alexandria formulated theories regarding God's mediation in the cosmos. Drawing on Neoplatonic ideas, these writers argued that God has contact with the world through divine agencies. Such a notion was subsequently expanded by rabbinic sages, who portrayed such intermediaries in various terms such as *Metatron* (Angel of the Presence), wisdom, and *Shekhinah* (Divine Presence).

Such theological reflection was far removed from the simple ecstatic experiences of the ancient Hebrews; in place of spiritual experience, these Jewish writers were preoccupied with the question how an Infinite God could become immanent in the world.

Within *aggadah* (early rabbinic literature) Jewish sages also engaged in theological speculation based on the biblical text. These doctrines were frequently of a secret nature; in a *midrash* (rabbinic commentary) on Genesis it is reported that these mystical traditions were repeated in a whisper so they would not be overheard by those for whom they were not intended. Thus, in the third century Rabbi Simeon ben Jehozedek asked Rabbi Samuel Nahman, 'Seeing that I have heard you are adept at *aggadah*, tell me how light was created.' He replied in a whisper, upon which the other sage retorted, 'Why do you tell this in a whisper, seeing that it is taught clearly in a scriptural verse?' The first sage responded, 'Just as I have myself had it whispered to me, even so I have whispered it to you'. (*Midrash Rabba* on Genesis 3). In the same century, Rabbi Judah, for example, said in the name of Rab that God's secret name could only be entrusted to one who is 'modest and meek, in the midway of life, not easily provoked to anger, temperate, and free from vengeful feelings' (*Talmud Kiddushin* 71a).

The first chapter of Ezekiel played an important role in early rabbinic mysticism. In this biblical text the *merkavah* (divine chariot) is described in detail, and this scriptural source served as the basis of rabbinic speculation about the nature of the Deity. It was the aim of the mystic to be a '*merkavah* rider', so that he would be able to penetrate the heavenly mysteries. Such mystics were known as the '*yorde merkavah*.' Within this contemplative system, the rabbis believed that the pious could free themselves from the fetters of bodily existence and enter paradise.

A further dimension of this theory was that certain pious individuals could temporarily ascend into the unseen realm and, having learnt the deepest secrets, return to earth. These mystics were able to attain a state of ecstasy, to behold visions and hear voices. As students of the *merkavah*, they were the ones able to attain the highest degree of spiritual insight. A description of these *merkavah* mystics is contained in *hekhalot* (heavenly hall) literature from the seventh to the eleventh centuries CE. In order to make their heavenly ascent, these mystics followed strict ascetic disciplines, including fasting, ablution and the invocation of God's name. After reaching a state of ecstasy, the mystic was able to enter the seven heavenly halls and attain a vision of the divine chariot.

Closely associated with this form of speculation was *maaseh bereshit* (mystical theories about creation). Within aggadic sources the rabbis discussed the hidden meanings of the Genesis narrative. The most important early treatise, possibly from the second century CE, which describes the process of creation is *Sefer Yetsirah* (The Book of Creation). According to this cosmological text, God created the universe by thirty-two mysterious paths, consisting of twenty-two letters of the Hebrew alphabet together with ten *sefirot* (divine emanations). Of these twenty-two letters we read: 'He hewed them, combined them, weighed them, interchanged them, and through them produced the whole creation and everything that is destined to come into being'. (*Sefer Yetsirah* 2.2).

These Hebrew letters are of three types: mothers, doubles and simples. The mothers (*aleph, mem, shin*) symbolize the three primordial elements of all existing things: water is symbolized by *mem* fire by *shin* and air by *aleph*. In the microcosm (the human form) these three mothers represent 'the head, the belly and the chest – the head from fire; the belly from water; and the chest from the air that lies in between' (*Sefer Yetsirah* 3.7).

In addition to these three mother letters, there are seven double letters in Hebrew (*beth, gimel, daleth, caph, peh, resh, tau*), which signify the contraries in the universe (forces that serve two mutually opposed ends). These letters were 'formed, designed, created and combined into the stars of the universe, the days of the week, and the orifices of perception in man . . . two eyes, two ears, two nostrils and a mouth through which he perceives by his senses' (*Sefer Yetsirah* 4.6-7). Finally there are twelve simple Hebrew letters (*hey, vav, zayin, chet, tet, yod, lamed, nun, samech, ayin, tsade, kof*), which correspond to the chief human activities – sight, hearing, smell, speech, desire for food, the sexual appetite, movement, anger, mirth, thought, sleep and work. The letters are also emblematic of the twelve signs of the zodiac in the heavenly sphere, the twelve months and the chief limbs of the body. Thus the individual, world and time are linked to one another through the process of creation by means of the Hebrew alphabet.

These recondite doctrines are supplemented by a theory of divine emanation through the ten *sefirot*. The first of the *sefirot* is the spirit of the living God; air is the second of the *sefirot* and is derived from the first. On it are hewn the twenty-two letters. The third of the *sefirot* is the water that comes from the air. The fourth of the *sefirot* is the fire that comes from water, through which God made the heavenly wheels, the seraphim and the ministering angels. The remaining six *sefirot* are the six dimensions of space: north, south, east, west, height and depth.

These ten *sefirot* are the moulds into which all created things were originally cast. They constitute form rather than matter. The twenty-two letters, on the other hand, are the prime cause of matter: everything that exists is due to the creative force of the Hebrew letters, but they receive their form from the *sefirot*. According to this cosmological doctrine, God transcends the universe – nothing exists outside him. The visible world is the result of the emanation of the divine, and God is the cause of the form and matter of the cosmos. By combining emanation and creation in this manner, the *Sefer Yetsirah* attempts to harmonize the concepts of divine immanence and transcendence. God is immanent in that the *sefirot* are an outpouring of his spirit, and he is transcendent in that the matter which was shaped into the forms is the product of his creative action. Such speculation served as the basis for later mystical reflection of the mediaeval period.

Hasidei Ashkenaz

The mystical text of early rabbinic Judaism was studied by Jewish settlers in the Rhineland from approximately the ninth century. During the twelfth and thirteenth centuries these authorities – the *Hasidei Ashkenaz* (pious men of Germany) delved into *hekhalot* (heavenly hall) literature, and the *Sefer Yetsirah* as well as the philosophical works of such scholars as Saadiah Gaon and various Spanish and Italian Jewish Neoplatonists. Among the greatest figures of this period were the twelfth-century Samuel ben Kalonymus of Speyer, his son Judah ben Samuel of Regensburg, who wrote the *Book of the Pious*, and Eleazar ben Judah of Worms, who composed the treatise *The Secret of Secrets*. Though the writings of these and other mystics were not systematic in character, their works do display a number of common characteristics.

In their writings these mystics were preoccupied with the mystery of divine unity. God himself, they believed, cannot be known by human reason – thus all anthropomorphic depictions of God in Scripture should be understood as referring to God's glory, which was formed out of *kavod* (divine fire). This *kavod* was revealed by God to the prophets and has been made manifest to mystics in different ways through the ages. The aim of German mysticism was to attain a vision of God's glory through the cultivation of the life of *hasiduth* (pietism), which embraced devotion, saintliness and contemplation. *Hasiduth* made the highest demands on the devotee in terms of humility and altruism. The ultimate sacrifice for these *hasidim* (pious ones) was *kiddush ha-Shem* (martyrdom), and during this period there were ample opportunities for Jews to die in this way as a result of Christian persecution. Allied to such a manifestation of selfless love of God was the emphasis on a profound sense of God's presence in the world; for these sages God's glory permeates all things.

Within this theological framework the concept of the *hasid* (pious one) was of paramount importance. To be a *hasid* was a religious ideal that transcended all intellectual attainments. The *hasid* was remarkable, not because of any scholarly qualities, but through his spiritual accomplishments. According to these scholars, the *hasid* must reject and overcome every temptation of ordinary life. Insults and shame must be endured. In addition, he should renounce worldly goods, mortify the flesh and do penance for any sins. Such an ascetic way of life against all obstacles would lead the devotee to the heights of true fear and love of God. In its most sublime form such fear was conceived of as identical with love and devotion, enabling joy to enter the soul.

In the earlier *merkavah* tradition the mystic was the keeper of holy mysteries. But for these German sages, humility and self-abnegation were the hallmarks of the authentic religious life. Allied with these personal characteristics, the *hasid* was perceived as capable of mastering magical powers. In the writings of Eleazar ben Judah of Worms, for example, are found tracts on magic and the effectiveness of God's secret names as well as recipes for creating the *golem* (an artificial man) through letter manipulation.

Another feature of this movement concerned prayer mysticism. In the literature of the pietists, attention was given to techniques of mystical speculation based on the calculation of the words in prayers, benedictions and hymns. The number of words in a prayer, as well as the numerical value, were linked to biblical passages of equal numerical value, as well as with the designations of God and the angels. Here prominence was given to the techniques of *gematria* (the calculation of the numerical value of Hebrew words and the search for connections with other words of equal value) and *notarikon* (the interpretation of the letters of a word as abbreviations of whole sentences).

According to these German *hasidim*, prayer was like Jacob's ladder extended from earth to heaven: it was a process of mystical ascent. It was in this milieu that the famous Hymn of Glory was composed – a prayer that subsequently gained a central place in the Ashkenazi liturgy. Here the ignorance of God is suffused with longing for intimacy with the Divine:

> Sweet hymns and songs will I recite,
> To sing to Thee by day and night,
> Of Thee who art my soul's delight.
>
> How doth my soul within me yearn,
> Beneath Thy shadow to return,
> The secret mysteries to learn.
>
> Thy glory shall my discourse be,
> In images I picture Thee,
> Although myself I cannot see.
>
> In mystic utterances alone,
> By prophet and by seer made known,
> Hast Thou Thy radiant glory shown.
>
> My meditation day and night,
> May it be pleasant in Thy sight,
> For Thou art my soul's delight.

For the *Hasidei Ashkenaz* such prayers as well as mystical practices and beliefs provided a means of consolation and escape from the miseries that beset the Rhineland communities during the twelfth and thirteenth centuries.

The Emergence of Kabbalah (Mystical Tradition)

Parallel with these developments in Germany, Jewish mystics in southern France were engaged in mystical speculation about the nature of God, the soul, the existence of evil and the religious life. In twelfth-century Provence the earliest kabbalistic text, the *Bahir* (*The Book of Light*) reinterpreted the concept of the *sefirot* as depicted in the *Sefer Yetsirah*. According to the *Bahir*, the *sefirot* were conceived of as vessels, crowns or words that constitute the structure of the divine realm. Basing themselves on this anonymous work, various Jewish sages of Provence engaged in similar mystical reflection. Isaac the Blind, the son of Abraham ben David of Posquières, conceived of the *sefirot* as emanations from a hidden dimension of the Godhead. Utilizing Neoplatonic ideas, he argued that out of the Infinite (*Ayn Sof*) emanated the first supernatural essence, divine thought, from which came the remaining *sefirot*. Beings in the world beneath, he believed, were materializations of the *sefirot* at lower degrees of reality. The purpose of mystical activity was to ascend the ladder of emanations to unite with divine thought.

In Gerona the traditions from Isaac the Blind were broadly disseminated. One of the most important of these Geronese kabbalists was Azriel of Gerona, who replaced divine thought with divine will, as the first emanation of the *Ayn Sof*. The most famous figure of this circle was Moses ben Nahman, known as Nahmanides, who helped this mystical school gain general acceptance. His involvement in kabbalistic speculation, combined with his halakhic (legal) authority, persuaded many Jews that mystical teachings were compatible with rabbinic Judaism. In his commentary on the Torah he frequently referred to kabbalistic notions to explain the true meaning of the text. In his discussion of sacrifice, for instance, Nahmanides stated that by means of the sacrifices blessing emanates to the higher powers. Here sacrifice is conceived of as providing emanations from the *sefirot*; it raises human desire in order to draw it near and unite it with the desire of the higher powers and then draws the higher desire and lower desire into one desire.

During the time that these Geronese mystics were propounding their kabbalistic theories, different mystical schools of thought developed in other parts of Spain. Influenced by the *Hasidei Ashkenaz* and the Sufi traditions of Islam, Abraham ben Samuel Abulafia wrote meditative texts on the technique of combining the letters of the alphabet as a means of realizing human aspirations towards prophecy. As an admirer of Moses Maimonides, he believed his system was a continuation and elaboration of the teaching of Maimonides' *The Guide for the Perplexed*.

Another Spanish kabbalist, Isaac ibn Latif, also attempted to elaborate ideas found in Maimonides' *Guide*. For ibn Latif, the primeval will was the source of all emanation. Adopting Neoplatonic conceptions, he argued that from the first created thing emanated all the other stages, referred to symbolically as light, fire, ether and water. Each of these, he believed, was the subject of a branch of wisdom: mysticism, metaphysics, astronomy and physics. According to ibn Latif, kabbalah was superior to philosophy – the highest intellectual understanding reaching only the 'back' of the Divine whereas the 'face' is disclosed only in supra-intellectual ecstasy. True prayer leads to communion with the active intellect, and then to union of the active intellect with the first created thing. Beyond this union is the union through thought, which was intended to reach the prime will and ultimately to stand before God himself.

Other Spanish kabbalists were more attracted to gnostic ideas. Isaac ha-Kohen, for example, elaborated the theory of a demonic emanation whose ten spheres were counterparts of the holy *sefirot*. The mingling of such gnostic teaching with the kabbalah of Gerona resulted in the publication of the major mystical work of Spanish Jewry, the *Zohar* (*The Book of Splendour*), composed by the thirteenth-century writer Moses ben Shem Tov de Leon in Guadalajara. Although the author placed the work in a setting of the second century CE, focusing on Rabbi Simeon bar Yochai and his disciples after the Bar Kokhba uprising, the doctrines of the *Zohar* are of a much later origin. Written in Aramaic, the text is largely a *midrash* in which the Torah is given a mystical or ethical interpretation.

God and Creation

According to these various kabbalistic systems God in himself lies beyond any speculative comprehension. To express the unknowable aspect of the Divine, early kabbalists of Provence and Spain referred to the divine Infinite as *Ayn Sof* – the absolute perfection in which there is no distinction or plurality. The *Ayn Sof* does not reveal itself; it is beyond all thought and at times is identified with the Aristotelian First Cause. In kabbalistic teaching, creation is bound up with the manifestation of the hidden God and his outward movement. According to the *Zohar*, the *sefirot* emanate from the hidden depths of the Godhead like a flame:

> Within the most hidden recess a dark flame issued from the mystery of the *Ayn Sof*, the Infinite, like a fog forming in the unformed – enclosed in a ring of that sphere, neither white nor black, neither red nor green, of no colour whatever. Only after this flame began to assume size and dimension, did it produce radiant colours. From the innermost centre of the flame sprang forth a well out of which colours issued and spread upon everything beneath, hidden in the mysterious hiddenness of *Ayn Sof.*

These *sefirot* emanate successively from above to below, each one revealing a stage in the process. The common order of the *sefirot* and the names most generally used are: (1) supreme crown, (2) wisdom, (3) intelligence, (4) greatness, (5) power (or judgement), (6) beauty (or compassion), (7) endurance, (8) majesty, (9) foundation (or righteous one), and (10) kingdom. These ten *sefirot* are formally arranged in threes. The first triad consists of the first three *sefirot* and constitutes the intellectual realm of the inner structure of the Divine. The second triad is composed of the next three *sefirot* from the psychic or moral level of the Godhead. Finally, the seventh, eighth and ninth *sefirot* represent the archetypes of certain forces in nature. The remaining *sefirah*, kingdom, constitutes the channel between the higher and the lower worlds. The ten *sefirot* together demonstrate how an infinite, undivided and unknowable God is the cause of all the modes of existence in the finite plane.

In their totality these *sefirot* are frequently represented as a cosmic tree of emanation. It grows from its root – the first *sefirah* – and spreads downwards in the direction of the lower worlds to those *sefirot* that constitute its trunk and its main branches. According to the *Bahir*, all the divine powers of the Holy One rest upon one another and are like a tree. Another depiction of the *sefirot* is in the form of a man: the first *sefirah* represents the head, the next three *sefirot* the cavities of the brain, the fourth and fifth *sefirot* the arms, the sixth the torso, the seventh and eighth the legs, the ninth the sexual organ, and the tenth the all-embracing totality of this image. In kabbalistic literature this heavenly man is also divided into two parts, the left column being made up of the female *sefirot* and the right column of the male. Another arrangement presents the *sefirot* as ten concentric circles, a depiction related to mediaeval cosmology in which the universe is understood to be made up of ten spheres.

For the kabbalists the *sefirot* are dynamically structured: through them divine energy flows from its source and separates into individual channels, reuniting in the lowest *sefirah*. These *sefirot* were also understood as divine substances as well as containers of God's essence; often they are portrayed as flames of fire. Yet despite their individuality, they are unified with the *Ayn Sof* in the moment of creation. According to the *Zohar*, all existences are emanations from the Deity – he is revealed in all things because he is immanent in them: He is separated from all things, and is at the same time not separated from all things. For all things are united in him, and he unites himself with all things. There is nothing which is not in him. In assuming a shape, he has given existence to all things.

To reconcile this process of emanation with the doctrine of creation *ex nihilo*, some kabbalists argued that the *Ayn Sof* should be seen as *ayin* (nothingness). Thus the manifestation of the Divine through the *sefirot* is a self-creation out of divine nothingness. Other kabbalists, however, maintained that creation does not occur within the Godhead. It takes place at a lower level, where created beings are formed independently of God's essence.

The Problem of Evil

For the kabbalists the existence of evil was a central issue. According to one tradition evil has no objective reality. Human beings are unable to receive all the influx from the *sefirot*, and it is this inability that is the origin of evil. Created beings are therefore estranged from the source of emanation and this results in the illusion that evil exists. Another view, as propounded in the *Bahir*, depicts the *sefirah* of power as 'an attribute whose name is evil'. On the basis of such a teaching Isaac the Blind concluded that there must be a positive root of evil and death. During the process of differentiation of forces below the *sefirot* evil became concretized. This interpretation led to the doctrine that the source of evil is the supra-abundant growth of the power of judgement – due to the separation and substitution of the attribute of judgement from its union with compassion. Pure judgement produced *sitra ahra* (the other side) from within itself, just as a vessel filled to overflowing spills its contents on the ground. The *sitra ahra* consists of the domain of emanations and demonic powers. Though it originated from one of God's attributes, it is not part of the divine realm.

In the *Zohar* there is a detailed hierarchical structure of this emanation, in which the *sitra ahra* is depicted as having ten *sefirot* of its own. The evil in the universe, the *Zohar* explains, has its origins in the leftovers of worlds that were destroyed. Another view in the *Zohar* is that the Tree of Life and the Tree of Knowledge were harmoniously bound together until Adam separated them, thereby bringing evil into the world. This event is referred to as the cutting of the shoots and is the prototype of sins in the Bible. Evil thus originated through human action. Both these views concerning the origin of evil are reconciled in another passage, where it is asserted that the disposition towards evil derives from the cosmic evil that is in the realm of the *sitra ahra*.

According to the *Zohar*, evil is like the bark of a tree of emanation; it is a husk or shell in which lower dimensions of existing things are encased. As the *Zohar* explains, 'When King Solomon went into the nut garden, he took a nut-shell and drew an analogy from its layers to these spirits which inspire sensual desires in human beings, as it is written, "and the delights of the sons of men are from male and female demons"' (Ecclesiastes 2:8). This verse also indicates that the pleasures in which men indulge during sleep give birth to multitudes of demons. 'The Holy One, blessed be he, found it necessary to create all things in the world to ensure its permanence, so that there should be, as it were, a brain with many membranes encircling it.'

In this context evil is understood as a waste product of an organic process – it is compared to bad blood, foul water, dross after gold has been refined and the dregs of wine. Yet despite this depiction, the *Zohar* asserts that there is holiness even in the *sitra ahra*, regardless of whether it was conceived as a result of the emanation of the last *sefirah* or as a consequence of sin. The domains of good and evil are intermingled and it is the individual's duty to separate them.

In explaining this picture of the divine creation, kabbalists adopted a Neoplatonic conception of a ladder of spiritual reality composed of four worlds in descending order. First is the domain of *atzilut* (emanation), consisting of the ten *sefirot* that form *Adam Kadmon* (primordial man). The second world, based on *hekhalot* literature, is the realm of *beriyah* (creation), which is made up of the Throne of Glory and the seven heavenly palaces. In the third world, *yetsirah* (formation), dwell most of the angels presided over by the angel Metatron. This is the scene of the seven heavenly halls guarded by angels to which *merkavah* mystics attempt to gain admission. In the fourth world of *asiyah* (making) are the lower order of angels – the *ophanim* who combat evil and receive prayers. This is the spiritual archetype of the material cosmos, heaven and the earthly world. *Asiyah* is both the last link in the divine chain of being and the domain where the *sitra ahra* is manifest; and in this realm the forces of good struggle with the demons.

The Soul

For mystics the doctrine of a hidden God who brings about creation had important implications for the kabbalistic view of humankind. The biblical idea that human beings were created in the image of God implies that they are modelled on the *sefirot*, and are microcosms reflecting the nature of the cosmos. Since the *sefirot* are reflected so, individuals are able to act as perfecting agents through their own lives and deeds. As far as souls are concerned, they are stored in one of the palaces in the sphere of *beriyah* (creation) where they are taught divine secrets. But when they enter the world of *asiyah* (making), such knowledge disappears. According to some kabbalists, the body that houses the soul is the work of the *sitra ahra* (the other side); others contend that corporeality is neither intrinsically good nor bad. On the other hand, there were those who saw bodily processes as reflecting heavenly processes – in such a context the sexual union was regarded as metaphysically significant.

The soul itself consists of three faculties. The lowest is the *nefesh* (the gross side of the soul) and it is the vital element that is the source of animation. From the *nefesh* springs all movement, instincts and physical desires. The next faculty is the *ruah* (spirit), which constitutes the moral element. Finally *neshamah* (super soul) is the rational component – it functions in the study of Torah and facilitates the apprehension of the Divine. These three dimensions of the soul derive from three *sefirot*: *neshamah*, being the soul in its most perfected state, emanates from the *sefirah* of wisdom; *ruah* from the *sefirah* of beauty; *nefesh* from the *sefirah* of foundation – it is the aspect of divinity that comes most into contact with the material universe. These three dimensions of the soul enable humans to fit into God's plan of creation and empower them with various duties to the cosmos, which is seen as a reflection of the heavenly realm. As the *Zohar* states:

> In these three (*neshamah, ruah*, and *nefesh*) we find an exact image of what is above in the celestial world. For all three form only one soul, one being, where all is one ... above the *nefesh* is the *ruah* which dominates the *nefesh*, imposes laws upon it and enlightens it as much as its nature requires. And then high above the *ruah* is the *neshamah* which in turn rules the *ruah* and sheds upon it the light of life.
>
> (*Zohar* 2:142)

After death the soul leaves the body for its ascent to the higher realms. It is only after death that the soul becomes conscious of the *neshamah*. For the kabbalists the *neshamah* must become pure and perfected in order to return to the Infinite from which it emanated. In this light the doctrine of transmigration of the soul becames an important element of the kabbalist system. According to the *Zohar*, 'All souls must undergo transmigration; and men do not understand the ways of the Holy One. They know not that they are brought before the tribunal both before they enter into this world and after they leave it. They know not the many transmigrations and hidden trials which they have to undergo' (*Zohar* 2:99). Such transmigration is required because the soul must reach the highest state of this evolution before it can return to its source. Related to this view is the Zoharic theory of the pre-existence of the body: 'At the moment when the earthly union takes place, the Holy One sends to earth a form resembling a man and bearing upon itself the divine seal' (*Zohar* 3:107).

Although the soul in its most exalted state can experience love in the union with the Infinite, it is possible to realize ecstatic love while the soul is in the body. One way to attain such realization is through serving God. The service of the Divine through love leads the soul to a union with its place of origin and gives a foretaste of what will occur at death. As the *Zohar* (2:216) explains, 'Whosoever serves God out of love comes into union with the holiness of the world which is to be.' Though such self-perfection of the soul is a major goal of earthly existence, the soul also has a central role in *tikkun*, the cosmic repair of the disharmony in the world that has resulted from Adam's sin. Through the cutting off of the *sefirah* kingdom from other *sefirot*, the *sitra ahara* attained dominance. Yet human beings can bring about *tikkun*, since their souls can ascend higher than the angels. As the *Zohar* explains, human action has a profound effect on the higher worlds: 'It is from below that the movement starts, and thereafter is all perfected. If the community of Israel failed to initiate the impulse, the One above also would not move to go to her, and it is thus the yearning from below which brings about the completion above.'

The Mystic Way

For the mystic, deeds of *tikkun* sustain the world, activate nature to praise God, and bring about the coupling of the tenth and sixth *sefirot*. Such repair is accomplished by keeping the commandments, which are conceived of as vessels for establishing contact with the Godhead and for ensuring divine mercy. Such a religious life provided the kabbalist with a means of integrating into the divine hierarchy of creation – the kabbalah was able to guide the soul back to its source in the Infinite.

The supreme rank attainable by the soul at the end of its sojourn is *devekut*, the mystical cleaving to God. The early kabbalists of Provence defined *devekut* as the goal of the mystic way. According to Isaac the Blind, 'The principal task of the mystics and of they who contemplate on his name is, "And you shall cleave to him" [Deuteronomy 13:4] and this is a central principle of the Torah and of prayer, and of blessings, to harmonize one's thought above, to conjoin God in his letters and to link the ten *sefirot* to him.' For Nahmanides *devekut* is a state of mind in which one constantly remembers God and his love 'to the point that when [a person] speaks with someone else, his heart is not with them at all but is still before God . . . whoever cleaves in this way to his Creator becomes eligible to receive the Holy Spirit.' According to Nahmanides, the true *hasid* is able to attain such a spiritual state. *Devekut* does not completely eliminate the distance between God and the individual – it denotes instead a state of beatitude and intimate union between the soul and its source.

In ascending the higher worlds, the path of prayer parallels the observance of God's commandments. Yet unlike the *mitzvot* (commandments), prayer is independent of action and can become a process of meditation. Mystical prayer accompanied by meditative *kavvanot* (intentions), focusing on each prayer's kabbalistic content, is a feature of the various systems of kabbalah. For the kabbalists prayer is seen as the ascent of the individual into the higher realms, where the soul could integrate with the higher spheres.

By using the traditional liturgy in a symbolic fashion, prayer repeats the hidden processes of the cosmos. At the time of prayer, the hierarchy of the upper realms is revealed as one of the names of God. Such disclosure is what constitutes the mystical activity of the individual in prayer, as the kabbalist concentrates on the name that belongs to the domain through which his prayer is passing. The *kavvanah* involved in mystic prayer is seen as a necessary element in the mystery of heavenly unification that brought the Divine down to the lowest realm and tied the *sefirot* to each other and the *Ayn Sof*. As the *Zohar* explains, 'Both upper and lower worlds are blessed through the man who performs his prayer in a union of action and word, and thus affects a unification.'

In addition to mystical meditation, the kabbalists made use of the letters of the alphabet and of the names of God for the purposes of meditative training. By engaging in the combination of letters and names, the mystic is able to empty his mind so as to concentrate on divine matters. Through such experiences the kabbalists believed they could attempt to conduct the soul to a state of the highest rapture in which divine reality is disclosed.

Lurianic Kabbalah

In the early modern period Safed in Israel had become a major centre of Jewish religious life. By the sixteenth century this small community had become a centre for the manufacture of cloth and had grown in size to a population of over 10,000 Jews. Here talmudic academies were established and small groups engaged in the study of kabbalistic literature as they piously awaited the coming of the Messiah. Heightened by the expulsion of Jews from Spain and

Portugal, such messianic expectation became a prevalent theme of religious poetry written in Safed during this period. The hymn composed by Solomon ha-Levy Alkabetz, 'Come, My Beloved', for instance, speaks of the Holy City as an abode for the Sabbath bride and the Davidic King: 'Come, my beloved, to meet the bride . . . O Sanctuary of our king, O city, arise, go forth from thy overthrow; long enough hast thou dwelt in the valley of weeping . . . shake thyself from the dust; arise, put on the garments of thy glory O my people.'

In this town mystics also participated in various ascetic practices such as fasting, public confessions of sins, wearing sackcloth and ashes, and praying at the graves of venerable sages. Such self-mortification was carried to an extreme by Abraham ha-Levi Beruchim, who wandered through the streets of Safed calling on people to repent; he then led those he attracted to the synagogue, climbed into a sack, and ordered these individuals to throw stones at him.

In this centre of kabbalistic activity one of the greatest mystics of Safed, Moses Cordovero, collected, organized and interpreted the teachings of earlier mystical authors. His work constitutes a systematic summary of the kabbalah up to his time, and in his most important treatise, *Pardes Rimonim* (*The Orchard of Pomegranates*), he outlines the zoharic concepts of the Godhead, the *sefirot*, the celestial powers and the earthly processes. In this study he describes the sefirot as vessels in which the light of the *Ayn Sof* is contained and through which it is reflected in different forms. For Cordovero the Godhead is manifest in every part of the finite world in this way. In another important work, *The Palm Tree of Deborah*, he expresses the notion that in order to achieve the highest degree of the religous life, one should not only observe the commandments but also imitate divine processes and patterns.

Later in the sixteenth century kabbalistic speculation was transformed by the greatest mystic of Safed, Isaac Luria. Originally brought up in Egypt where he studied the Talmud and engaged in business, Luria withdrew to an island in the Nile where he meditated on the *Zohar* for seven years. In 1569 he arrived in Safed and died three years later, after having passed on his teaching to a small group of disciples. Of primary importance in the Lurianic system is the mystery of creation. In the literature of early kabbalists creation was understood as a positive act: the will to create was awakened within the Godhead, and this resulted in a long process of emanation. For Luria, however, creation is a negative event: the *Ayn Sof* had to bring into being an empty space in which creation could occur, since divine light was everywhere, leaving no room for creation to take place. Thus creation was accomplished by the process of *tzimtzum* – the contraction of the Godhead into itself, and therefore the first act was not positive, but rather one that demanded withdrawal. God had to go into exile from the *tehiru* (empty space), so that the process of creation could be initiated. *Tzimtzum* therefore postulates divine exile at the first step of creation.

After this act of withdrawal, a line of light flowed from the Godhead into the *tehiru* and took on the shape of the *sefirot* in the form of *Adam Kadmon*, the primordial man. In this process divine lights created the vessels – the external shapes of the *sefirot* – which gave specific characteristics to each divine emanation. Yet these vessels were not strong enough to contain such pure light and they shattered. This *shevirat ha-kelim* (breaking of the vessels) brought disaster and upheaval to the emerging emanations: the lower vessels broke down and fell, the three highest emanations were damaged, and the empty space was divided into two parts. The first part consisted of the broken vessels with many divine sparks clinging to them, and the second part was the upper realm where the pure light of God escaped to preserve its purity.

In explaining the purpose of the *tzimtzum*, Luria points out that the *Ayn Sof* before creation was not completely unified – there were elements in it that were potentially different from the rest of the Godhead. The *tzimtzum* separated these different elements from one another. After this contraction occurred *reshimu* (a residue) was left behind which was like water clinging to a bucket after it has been emptied. This residue included different elements that were part of the Godhead, and after the withdrawal, they were poured out into the empty space. Thus the separation of different elements from the Godhead was accomplished. The reason for the emanation of the divine powers and the formation of *Adam Kadmon* was the attempt to integrate these now separate elements into the scheme of creation and thereby transform them into co-operative forces. Their task was to create the vessels of the *sefirot* into which the divine lights would flow. But the breaking of the vessels was a rebellion of these different elements, a refusal to participate in the process of creation. And by this rebellious act they were able to attain a realm of their own in the lower part of the *tehiru*; after the breaking of the vessels, these elements expressed themselves as the powers of evil.

Following the shattering of the vessels the cosmos was divided into two parts – the kingdom of evil in the lower part and the realm of divine light in the upper part. For Luria evil is seen as opposed to existence, and therefore it is not able to exist by its own power. Instead it has to derive spiritual force from the divine light. This is accomplished by keeping captive the sparks of the divine light that fell when the vessels were broken; and these subsequently gave sustenance to the satanic realm.

Divine attempts to bring unity to all existence now had to focus on the struggle to overcome the evil forces. This was achieved by a continuing process of divine emanation, which at first created the *sefirot*, the sky, the earth, the Garden of Eden and human beings. The individual human being was intended to serve as the battle-ground for this conflict between good and evil. In this regard Adam reflected symbolically the dualism in the cosmos – he possessed a sacred soul while his body represented the evil forces. God's intention was that Adam should defeat the evil within himself and bring about Satan's downfall. But when Adam failed a catasrophe occurred parallel to the breaking of the vessels; instead of divine sparks being saved and uplifted, many new divine lights fell and evil became stronger.

Rather than relying on the action of one person, God then chose the people of Israel to vanquish evil and raise up the captive sparks. The Torah was given to symbolize the Jews' acceptance of this allotted task. When the ancient Israelites undertook to keep the law, redemption seemed imminent. Yet the people of Israel then created the golden calf, a sin parallel to Adam's disobedience. Again divine sparks fell and the forces of evil were renewed. For Luria, history is a record of attempts by the powers of good to rescue these sparks and unite the divine and earthly spheres. Luria and his disciples believed they were living in the final stages of this last attempt to overcome evil, in which the coming of the Messiah would signify the end of the struggle.

Related to the contraction of God, the breaking of the vessels and the exiled sparks, is Luria's conception of *tikkun*. For Lurianic mystics, this concept refers to the mending of what was broken during the *shevirat ha-kelim*. After the catastrophe in the divine realm the process of restoration began and every disaster was seen as a setback in this process. In this battle, keeping God's commandments is understood as contributing to repair – the divine sparks that fell can be redeemed by ethical and religious deeds. According to Luria, a spark is attached to all prayers and moral acts; if a Jew keeps the ethical and religious law these sparks are redeemed and lifted up. When the process is complete, evil will disappear. But every time a Jew sins a spark is captured and plunges into the satanic abyss. Every deed or misdeed thus has cosmic significance in the system of Lurianic kabbalah.

The Mystical Messiah

By the beginning of the seventeenth century Lurianic mysticism had made a major impact on Sephardic Jewry, and messianic expectations had also become a central feature of Jewish life. In this milieu the arrival of a self-proclaimed messianic king, Shabbatai Zevi, brought about a transformation of Jewish life and thought. Born in Smyrna into a wealthy family, Shabbatai had received a traditional Jewish education and later engaged in study of the *Zohar*. After leaving Smyrna in the 1650s he spent ten years in various cities in Greece as well as in Constantinople and Jerusalem. Eventually he became part of a kabbalistic group in Cairo and travelled to Gaza where he encountered Nathan Benjamin Levi, who believed Shabbatai was the Messiah. In 1665 his Messiahship was proclaimed, and Nathan sent letters to Jews in the Diaspora asking them to repent and recognize Shabbatai Zevi as their redeemer. Shabbatai, he announced, would take the Sultan's crown, bring back the lost tribes and inaugurate the period of messianic redemption.

After a brief sojourn in Jerusalem, Shabbatai went to Smyrna, where he encountered strong opposition on the part of some local rabbis. In response, he denounced the disbelievers and declared that he was the Anointed of the God of Jacob. This action evoked a hysterical response – a number of Jews fell into trances and had visions of him on a royal throne crowned as King of Israel. In 1666 he journeyed to Constantinople, but on the order of the grand vizier he was arrested and put into prison. Within a short time the prison quarters became a messianic court; pilgrims from all over the world made their way to Constantinople to join the messianic rituals and ascetic activities. In addition, hymns were written in his honour and new festivals were introduced. According to Nathan, who remained in Gaza, the alteration in Shabbatai's moods, from illumination to withdrawal, symbolized his souls' struggle with demonic powers; at times he was imprisoned by *kelippot* (the powers of evil) but at other moments he prevailed against them.

The same year Shabbatai spent three days with the Polish kabbalist, Nehemiah ha-Kohen, who later denounced him to the Turkish authorities. Shabbatai was brought to court and given the choice between conversion and death. In the face of this choice, he converted to Islam and took on the name Mehemet Effendi. Such an act of apostasy scandalized most of his followers, but he defended himself by asserting that he had become a Muslim in obedience to God's commands. Many of his followers accepted this explanation and refused to give up their belief. Some thought it was not Shabbatai who had become a Muslim, but rather a phantom who had taken on his appearance; the Messiah himself had ascended to heaven. Others cited biblical and rabbinic sources to justify Shabbatai's action. Nathan explained that the messianic task involved taking on the humiliation of being portrayed as a traitor to his people. Furthermore, he argued on the basis of Lurianic kabbalah that there were two kinds of divine light – a creative light and another light opposed to the existence of anything other than the *Ayn Sof*. While creative light formed structures of creation in the empty space, the other light became the power of evil after the *tzimtzum* (divine contraction). According to Nathan, the soul of the Messiah had been struggling against the power of evil from the beginning; his purpose was to allow divine light to penetrate this domain and bring about cosmic repair. In order to do this, the soul of the Messiah was not obliged to keep the law, but was free to descend into the abyss to liberate sparks and thereby conquer evil. In this light Shabbatai's conversion to Islam was explicable.

After Shabbatai's act of apostasy, Nathan visited him in the Balkans and then travelled to Rome, where he performed secret rites to bring about the end of the papacy. Shabbatai remained in Adrianople and Constantinople, where he lived as both Muslim and Jew. In 1672 he was deported to Albania where he disclosed his own kabbalistic teaching to his supporters. After he died in 1676, Nathan declared that Shabbatai had ascended to the supernal world. Eventually a number of groups continued in their belief that Shabbatai was the messiah, including a sect, the *Doenmeh* (Dissidents), which professed Islam publicly but nevertheless adhered to its own traditions. Marrying among themselves, the members of the sect eventually evolved into antinomian sub-groups that violated Jewish sexual laws and asserted the divinity of Shabbatai and their leader, Baruchiah Russo. In Italy several Shabbatean groups also emerged and propagated their views.

In the eighteenth century the most important Shabbatean sect was led by Jacob Frank, who was influenced by the *Doenmeh* in Turkey. Believing himself to be the incarnation of Shabbatai, Frank announced that he was the second person of the Trinity and gathered together a circle of disciples who indulged in licentious orgies. In the 1750s disputes took place between traditional Jews and

Frankists; subsequently Frank expressed his willingness to become a Christian but he wished to maintain his own group. This request was refused by Church leaders, yet Frank and his disciples were baptized. The clergy, however, became aware that Frank's Trinitarian beliefs were not consonant with Christian doctrine, and he was imprisoned in 1760 for thirteen years. Frank then settled in Germany, where he continued to subscribe to a variant of the Shabbatean kabbalistic tradition.

The Rise of Hasidism

By the middle of the eighteenth century the Jewish community had suffered numerous waves of persecution and was deeply dispirited by the conversion of Shabbatai Zevi. In this environment the Hasidic movement – grounded in *kabbalah* – sought to revitalize Jewish life. Following the massacres of the previous century, many Polish Jews became disenchanted with rabbinic Judaism and through Hasidism sought individual salvation by means of religious pietism. The founder of this new movement was Israel ben Eleazer, known as the Baal Shem Tov (or Besht). According to tradition, Israel ben Eleazer was born in southern Poland and in his twenties journeyed with his wife to the Carpathian mountains. In the 1730s he travelled to Mezibozh where he performed various miracles and instructed his disciples about kabbalistic lore. By the 1740s he had attracted a considerable number of disciples. After his death in 1760, Dov Baer of Mezhirich became the leader of this sect and Hasidism spread to southern Poland, the Ukraine and Lithuania.

The growth of this movement engendered considerable hostility on the part of rabbinic authorities. In particular the rabbinic leadership of Vilna issued an edict of excommunication; the *Hasidim* were charged with permissiveness in their observance of the commandments, laxity in the study of the Torah, excess in prayer, and preference for the Lurianic rather than the Ashkenazic prayerbook. In subsequent years the *Hasidim* and the *Mitnagdim* (their opponents) bitterly denounced one another. Relations deteriorated further when Jacob Joseph of Polonnoye published a book critical of the rabbinate; his work was burned and in 1781 the *Mitnagdim* ordered all relations with the *Hasidim* cease. By the end of the century the Jewish religious establishment of Vilna denounced the *Hasidim* to the Russian government, an act that resulted in the imprisonment of several leaders. Despite such condemnation, the Hasidic movement was eventually recognized by the Russian and Austrian governments; in the ensuing years the movement divided into a number of separate groups under different leaders who passed on positions of authority to their descendants.

Hasidism initiated a profound change in Jewish religious pietism. In the medieval period, the *Hasidei Ashkenaz* attempted to achieve perfection through various mystical activities. This tradition was carried on by Lurianic kabbalists who engaged in various forms of self-mortification. In opposition to such ascetic practices, the Besht and h.s followers emphasized the omnipresence of God rather than the shattering of the vessels and the imprisonment of divine sparks by the powers of evil. For Hasidic Judaism there is no place where God is absent; the doctrine of the *tzimtzum* was interpreted by Hasidic sages as only an apparent withdrawal of the divine presence. Divine light, they believed, is everywhere. As the Besht explained: in every human trouble, physical or spiritual, even in this trouble, God himself is there.

For some *Hasidim*, *devekut* (cleaving to God) in prayer was understood as the annihilation of selfhood and the ascent of the soul to divine light. In this context, joy, humility, gratitude, and spontaneity are seen as essential features of Hasidic worship. The central obstacles to concentration in prayer are distracting thoughts; according to Hasidism such sinful intentions contain a divine spark which can be released. In this regard, the traditional kabbalistic stress on theological speculation has been replaced by a preoccupation with mystical psychology, in which inner bliss is conceived of as the highest aim, rather than repair of the cosmos. For the Beshtian *Hasidim* it was also possible to achieve *devekut* in daily activities including drinking, business affairs, and sex. Such ordinary acts became religious if in performing them one cleaves to God, and *devekut* is thus attainable by all Jews rather than a scholarly elite. Unlike the earlier mystical tradition, Hasidism provided a means by which ordinary Jews could reach a state of spiritual ecstasy. Hasidic worship embraced singing, dancing and joyful devotion in anticipation of the period of messianic redemption.

Another central feature of this new movement was the institution of the *zaddik* (holy individual) or *rebbe* (spiritual leader), which gave expression to a widespread disillusionment with rabbinic leadership. According to Hasidism, the *zaddikim* were spiritually superior individuals who had attained the highest level of *devekut*. The goal of the *zaddik* was to elevate the souls of his flock to the divine light; his tasks included pleading to God for his people, immersing himself in their everyday affairs, and counselling and strengthening them.

As an authoritarian figure the *zaddik* was seen by his followers as possessing miraculous power to ascend to the divine realm. In this context *devekut* to God involved cleaving to the *zaddik*.

Given the emphasis on the role of the *rebbe*, Hasidic literature included summaries of the spiritual and kabbalistic teachings of various famous *zaddikim*, as well as stories about their miraculous deeds. Foremost among these leading figures was Zusya of Hanipol, Shneur Zalman of Liady, Levi Yitzhak of Berdichev, and Nahman of Bratslav. These various leaders developed their own customs, doctrines and music, and gathered around themselves disciples who made pilgrimages to their courts in the Ukraine and Polish Galicia. In central Poland Hasidism emphasized the centrality of faith and talmudic study; Lubavich *Hasidim* in Lithuania, on the other hand, combined kabbalistic speculation and rabbinic scholarship. From its inception at the end of the eighteenth century to the present day, this movement has kept alive the mystical tradition of the Jewish past.

Contemporary Kabbalah

Despite the growth and development of kabbalah amongst *Hasidim*, during the Jewish Enlightenment in the nineteenth century there was considerable opposition to practical kabbalah amongst modernizers who viewed traditional Jewish mystical teachings as irrelevant in contemporary society. Only a few circles of kabbalists were active outside Hasidic circles, such as the followers of Rabbi Yehuda Ashlag who composed a detailed commentary on the *Zohar* in the first half of the twentieth century. The modern study of Jewish mysticism, however, was promoted by Gershom Scholem, who created a new interest in kabbalistic lore. Scholem's works have been published in a variety of languages and have had a lasting influence on a wide number of readers.

Today traditionalists view themselves as students of the kabbalistic tradition of previous generations; yet, in the latter half of the last century, there has been a renewed fascination with kabbalah amongst young Jews who were part of the counterculture movement. In the 1960s a Jewish counter-culture emerged out of the general protest movement in the United States. A spiritual strand of counterculture was manifest amongst the followers of the former Lubavitcher rabbis Zalman Schachter-Shalomi and Shlomo Carlebach. During this period Rabbi Carlebach founded the House of Love and Prayer in San Francisco in 1967. This type of counterculture Judaism sought to combine communal life with a minimum of religious observance and a maximum of celebration including singing and dancing. One of the activites of this organization was the publication of the magazine *The Holy Beggar's Gazette*.

The unaffiliated fringe associated with Jewish counterculture consisted of artists and poets, many of whom were influenced by kabbalistic teachings. Although all the streams of the Jewish counterculture were interested in Jewish mysticism, the counterculture kabbalists reclaimed magical, heretical, and heterodox traditions. This approach is illustrated in Jerome Rothenberg's anthology, *A Big Jewish Book* and in David Meltzer's kabbalistic journal *Tree*. Meltzer also published *Tree Books* in which he made available the work of various Jewish poets; his magazine also included texts on Jewish mysticism, including the writings of Abraham Abulafia. Meltzer and his followers were particularly fascinated by Jewish letter mysticism, Jewish letter permuations and the *golem*. Jewish mystical traditions were also linked to certain trends in contemporary American poetry, as in Hirschman's *Black Alpha*.

Such a counterculture marked the beginning of popular interest in kabbalah as evidenced by Rabbi Herbert Wiener's *9 1/2 Mystics* which depicts the quest for an authentic form of Jewish mysticism. Other books by Charles Ponce and Perle Epstein similarly provided popular, nonacademic introductions to kabbalah for a wide audience. In the 1980s and 1990s such an interest in kabbalistic ideas intensified. Writings on Jewish mysticism are now available in the esoteric sections of most bookshops. These works typically psychologize mystical teachings and employ kabbalah as an instrument for balancing one's personality.

In the 1990s kabbalistic centres sprang up throughout the United States. Rav Berg's Kabbalah Centre has become increasingly important through the involvement of celebrities such as Madonna, who became fascinated with a New Age version of kabbalah. In New York Makor on the Upper West Side offers courses such as 'Inner Torah', 'Jewish Meditation: A Path for Self-Discovery', and 'Drop-in Kabbalah and Spirituality' – all of these courses emphasize the appicability of their teachings to modern life. Another central focus of pop kabbalah has been the magical use of kabbalah, and its association with astrology, palm reading, and face reading. Other exponents of kabbalistic techniques explore the connection between Judaism and spiritual practices including yoga. The Kabbalah Centre in New York, for example, offers courses in 'Basic Reincarnation.'

Not suprisingly 'pop kabbalah' has evoked widespread criticism from the Jewish establishment. The Toronto Vaad HaRabonim (rabbinic council) and the Queens' Vaad HaRabonim, for example, have issued statements to the public about avoiding the learning that takes place in Kabbalah Centres as well as purchasing books dealing with the subject. The Chief Rabbi and the *Bet Din* (religious court) of Johannesburg and the Rabbinical Association of South Africa have issued decrees of condemnation against the Kabbalah Centre with its various branches in New York, California and Florida as well as international centres in Israel, South America, and Europe under the directorship of Rabbi Philip Berg. Canadian rabbi Emanuel Schochet, a rabbinic authority on Jewish mysticism, has alleged that Rabbi Berg engages in acts of extortion by scaring people with various forms of evil and curses if they refuse to offer money to the Kabbalah Centre. In Schochet's view, the Kabbalah Centre makes ludicrous promises of physical health and wealth. Yet, despite such criticisms, New Age kabbalah continues to grow in popularity and currently exerts an important spiritual impact on its adherents.

1 The Bible and Early Rabbinic Period *c.*1900 BCE–*c.*CE 900

Introduction

The history of Jewish mysticism originates with God's encounter with the ancient Israelites. In the book of Genesis God called Abraham to depart from Ur and travel to Canaan. Abraham's dedication was afterwards tested by God's command that he sacrifice his son Isaac; only when a divine messenger ordered Abraham to desist was Isaac's life saved. Subsequently God revealed himself to Jacob and decreed that his name become Israel. Several hundred years later God appeared to Moses, calling him to free the Jewish people from Egyptian bondage. On the way through the desert God revealed his law to Moses on Mount Sinai – this encounter served as the basis for the evolution of the Jewish legal tradition. In the following centuries God appeared to the prophets through direct communications, visions and dreams; in this way he made himself manifest to his chosen people through their sojourn in the Promised Land and in exile.

With the cessation of prophecy, Jewish writers struggled to comprehend the nature and activity of God, such philosophers as Philo attempting to explain God's relation to the world. Similarly rabbinic scholars formulated the doctrine of a divine agent, Metatron, who was believed to mediate between God and the cosmos. Paralleling this doctrine the rabbis viewed wisdom as a channel of divine indwelling presence. Given this background of theological speculation, rabbinic sages also formulated mystical theories about creation.

ABRAHAM'S CALL

According to the Bible, Abraham, who lived at some point between the nineteenth and sixteenth centuries BCE, was the father of the Jewish people. Originally known as Abram, he came from Ur of the Chaldaeans, a Sumerian city of Mesopotamia. Together with his father Terah, his wife Sarai, and his nephew Lot, he travelled to Haran, a trading centre in northern Syria. There his father died, and God called upon him to go to Canaan. Here in this disclosure was the beginning of a chain of encounters with the Divine stretching over a millennium in the history of the nation.

Now the Lord said to Abram, 'Go from your country and your kindred and your father's house to the land that I will show you. And I will make of you a great nation, and make your name great, so that you will be a blessing. I will bless those who bless you, and him who curses you I will curse; and through you all the families of the earth shall bless themselves.' (Genesis 12:1–3)

THE SACRIFICE OF ISAAC

Not only did God speak directly to the Patriarchs, he also disclosed his will to them through divine messengers. After the birth of Abraham's son Isaac, God tested Abraham's dedication by ordering him to sacrifice Isaac, only telling him through a heavenly intermediary to desist at the last moment. The account of Abraham's trial and his faith in God has served as a source of inspiration to the Jewish people through centuries of persecution and tragedy.

After these things God tested Abraham, and said to him, 'Abraham!' And he said, 'Here am I.' He said, 'Take your son, your only son Isaac, whom you love, and go to the land of Moriah, and offer him there as a burnt offering upon one of the mountains of which I shall tell you.' So Abraham rose early in the morning, saddled his ass, and took two of his young men with him, and his son Isaac; and he cut the wood for the burnt offering, and arose and went to the place of which God had told him.

On the third day Abraham lifted up his eyes and saw the place afar off. Then Abraham said to his young men, 'Stay here with the ass; I and the lad will go yonder and worship, and come again to you.' And Abraham took the wood of the burnt offering, and laid it on Isaac his son; and he took in his hand the fire and the knife. So they went both of them together. And Isaac said to his father

Abraham, 'My father!' And he said, 'Here am I, my son.' He said, 'Behold, the fire and the wood; but where is the lamb for a burnt offering?' Abraham said, 'God will provide himself the lamb for a burnt offering, my son.' So they went both of them together.

When they came to the place of which God had told him, Abraham built an altar there, and laid the wood in order, and bound Isaac his son, and laid him on the altar, upon the wood. Then Abraham put forth his hand and took the knife to slay his son. But the angel of the Lord called to him from heaven, and he said, 'Abraham, Abraham!' And he said, 'Here am I.' He said, 'Do not lay your hand on the lad or do anything to him; for now I know that you fear God, seeing you have not withheld your son, your only son, from me.' (Genesis 22:1–13)

JACOB'S DREAM

In addition to direct communications and disclosures through divine messengers, God revealed himself to the Patriarchs through dreams. Thus when Jacob, who lived at some point between the nineteenth and sixteenth centuries BCE, fled from his brother Esau to Haran, he had a vision of a ladder rising to heaven and heard God speak to him promising that his offspring would inherit the land and fill the earth. This image of a ladder ascending heavenwards became a symbol in later Jewish thought for the heavenly ascent of the soul to the divine realm.

And he came to a certain place, and stayed there that night, because the sun had set. Taking one of the stones of the place, he put it under his head and lay down in that place to sleep. And he dreamed that there was a ladder set up on the earth, and the top of it reached to heaven; and behold, the angels of God were ascending and descending on it! And behold the Lord stood above it and said, 'I am the Lord, the God of Abraham your father and the God of Isaac: the land on which you lie I will give to you and your descendants.' (Genesis 28:11–13)

JACOB AND THE ANGEL

In Scripture God's encounter with his servants also took a more concrete form, as in the case of Jacob's confrontation with an angel at the gorge of the river Jabbok where God bestowed upon him his new name 'Israel'. Here Jacob is depicted as wrestling with a man – yet this person is later designated as God himself. For this reason Jacob called the name of the place 'Peniel' (the face of God) since there he saw God face to face.

And Jacob was left alone; and a man wrestled with him until the breaking of the day. When the man saw that he did not prevail against Jacob, he touched the hollow of his thigh; and Jacob's thigh was put out of joint as he wrestled with him. Then he said, 'Let me go, for the day is breaking.' But Jacob said, 'I will not let you go, unless you bless me.' And he said to him, 'What is your name?' And he said, 'Jacob.' Then he said, 'Your name shall no more be called Jacob, but Israel for you have striven with God and with men, and have prevailed.' (Genesis 32:24–8)

Moses and the Burning Bush

In the book of Exodus, God appeared to Moses out of a burning bush, commanding that he deliver the chosen people from Pharaoh's harsh bondage – in this mysterious disclosure God declared that the place where Moses stood was holy ground because of his presence there.

And the angel of the Lord appeared to him in a flame of fire out of the midst of a bush; and he looked, and lo, the bush was burning, yet it was not consumed. And Moses said, 'I will turn aside and see this great sight, why the bush is not burnt.' When the Lord saw that he turned aside to see, God called to him out of the bush, 'Moses, Moses!' And he said, 'Here am I.' Then he said, 'Do not come near; put your shoes from your feet for the place on which you are standing is holy ground.' (Exodus 3:2–5)

The Revelation on Mount Sinai

After the ancient Israelites had escaped from Egypt, they entered the wilderness of Sinai where Moses performed miracles to provide them with food and water. After travelling for ninety days, they encamped before Mount Sinai where God promised Moses that the Israelites would be his special people if they obeyed his commands. On the third day they came to the foot of the mountain amongst thunder, lightning and the sound of the ram's horn to hear God's voice.

On the morning of the third day there were thunders and lightnings, and a thick cloud upon the mountain, and a very loud trumpet blast, so that all the people who were in the camp trembled. Then Moses brought the people out of the camp to meet God; and they took their stand at the foot of the mountain. And Mount Sinai was wrapped in smoke, because the Lord descended upon it in fire; and the smoke of it went up like the smoke of a kiln, and the whole mountain quaked greatly. And as the sound of the trumpet grew louder and louder, Moses spoke, and God answered him in thunder. (Exodus 19:16–19)

MOSES AND THE TENT OF MEETING

Moses' intimacy with God was reflected in his encounter in the Tent of Meeting – there God spoke to him face to face as a man speaks to his friend. Among the prophets of Israel only Moses was granted such a divine disclosure. For this reason, the medieval Jewish philosopher Moses Maimonides declared that one of the central principles of the Jewish faith is that Moses was the greatest of the prophets.

Now Moses used to take the tent and pitch it outside the camp, far off from the camp; and he called it the tent of meeting. And every one who sought the Lord would go out to the tent of meeting, which was outside the camp. Whenever Moses went out to the tent, all the people rose up, and every man stood at his tent door, and looked after Moses, until he had gone into the tent. When Moses entered the tent, the pillar of cloud would descend and stand at the door of the tent, and the Lord would speak with Moses. And when all the people saw the pillar of cloud standing at the door of the tent, all the people would rise up and worship, every man at his tent door. Thus the Lord used to speak to Moses face to face, as a man speaks to his friend. (Exodus 33:7–11)

MOSES AND GOD'S GLORY

In a mysterious passage Moses pleaded with God to show him his ways so that he would know him and find grace in his sight. In response, God told him to stand in the cleft of a rock. There, God declared, he would cover him with his hand until he had passed by. Then, Moses would be able to see God's back, but not his face – through the centuries Jewish sages have reflected on the nature of this strange revelation.

Moses said to the Lord, 'See, thou sayest to me, "Bring up this people"; but thou hast not let me know whom thou wilt send with me. Yet thou hast said, "I know you by name, and you have also found favour in my sight." Now therefore, I pray thee, if I have found favour in thy sight, show me now thy ways, that I may know thee, and find favour in thy sight. Consider too that this nation is thy people.' And he said, 'My presence will go with you, and I will give you rest.' And he said to him, 'If thy presence will not go with me, do not carry us up from here. For how shall it be known that I have found favour in thy sight, I and thy people? Is it not in thy going with us so that we are distinct, I and thy people, from all the other people that are upon the face of the earth?' And the Lord said to Moses, 'This very thing that you have spoken I will do; for you have found favour in my sight, and I know you by name.' Moses said, 'I pray thee, show me thy glory.' And he said, 'I will make all my goodness pass before you, and proclaim before you my name, "The Lord"; and I will be gracious to whom I will be gracious, and will show mercy on whom I will show mercy. But,' he said, 'you cannot see my face; for man shall not see me and live.' And the Lord said, 'Behold there is a place by me where you shall stand upon the rock; and when my glory passes by I will put you in a cleft of the rock, and I will cover you with my hand until I have passed by; then I will take away my hand, and you shall see my back; but my face shall not be seen.' (Exodus 33:12–23)

Elijah and God's Revelation

Like Moses, the prophet Elijah received God's disclosure on a mountain top. Despairing that he was the sole prophet of the Lord, he experienced God's presence in a still small voice, rather than in natural phenomena as did Moses and the children of Israel. Thus, in the place where God made himself known to Moses, he speaks to Elijah out of the stillness.

And he arose, and ate and drank, and went in the strength of that food forty days and forty nights to Horeb the mount of God. And there he came to a cave, and lodged there; and behold, the word of the Lord came to him, and he said to him, 'What are you doing here, Elijah?' He said, 'I have been very jealous for the Lord, the God of hosts; for the people of Israel have forsaken thy covenant, thrown down thy altars, and slain thy prophets with the sword; and I, even I only, am left; and they seek my life, to take it away.' And he said, 'Go forth, and stand upon the mount before the Lord', but the Lord was not in the wind; and after the wind an earthquake. But the Lord was not in the earthquake; and after the earthquake a fire, but the Lord was not in the fire, and after the fire a still small voice. (1 Kings 19:11–12)

Isaiah's Vision in the Temple

From the eighth century BCE a series of prophets emerged who rebuked the people for their iniquity. Differentiating themselves from the bands of prophets who roamed through the land, these figures declared they had been sent by God to warn the people of impending disaster. In a mystical vision in the Temple, God is depicted as calling the prophet Isaiah to rebuke the people. Here Isaiah's vision is of a heavenly throne surrounded by flaming seraphim.

In the year that King Uzziah died I saw the Lord sitting upon a throne, high and lifted up; and his train filled the temple. Above him stood the Seraphim; each had six wings: with two he covered his face, and with two he covered his feet, and with two he flew. And one called to another and said:

> Holy, holy, holy is the Lord of hosts;
> the whole earth is full of his glory.

And the foundations of the thresholds shook at the voice of him who called, and the house was filled with smoke. And I said: 'Woe is me! For I am lost, for I am a man of unclean lips, and I dwell in the midst of a people of unclean lips; for my eyes have seen the King, the Lord of hosts!'

Then flew one of the Seraphim to me, having in his hand a burning coal which he had taken with tongs from the altar. And he touched my mouth, and said: 'Behold, this has touched your lips; your guilt is taken away, and your sin is forgiven.' And I heard the voice of the Lord saying, 'Whom shall I send, and who will go for us?' Then I said, 'Here am I! Send me.' (Isaiah 6:1–8)

Ezekiel's Vision of a Chariot

The post-exilic prophets encouraged the people not to give up hope. God, they declared, would deliver the fallen nation and gather them up again. This message of consolation was revealed to the prophet Ezekiel in a vision of a divine chariot (merkavah). As Ezekiel gazed over the plain, he saw what appeared to be an approaching storm with thunder, lightning and black clouds. Then he made out the figures of four angelic creatures standing wing-tip to wing-tip. At the centre a fire glowed and above under the blue vault of heaven was the Lord in human form circled by a rainbow. Beside each four-faced cherub was a whirling wheel full of eyes:

In the thirteenth year, in the fourth month, on the fifth day of the month, as I was among the exiles by the river Chebar, the heavens were opened, and I saw visions of God . . . As I looked, behold a stormy wind came out of the north, and a great cloud, with the brightness round about it, and fire flashing forth continually, and in the mist of the fire, as it were gleaming bronze. And from the midst of it came the likeness of four living creatures.

And this was their appearance: they had the form of men, but each had four faces, and each of them had four wings. Their legs were straight, and the soles of their feet were like the sole of a calf's foot; and they sparkled like burnished bronze. Under their wings on their four sides they had human hands. And the four had their faces and their wings thus: their wings touched one another; they went every one straight forward, without turning as they went.

As for the likeness of their faces, each had the face of a man in front; the four had the face of a lion on the right side, the four had the face of an ox on the left side, and the four had the face of an eagle at the back. Such were their faces. And their wings were spread out above; each creature had two wings, each of which touched the wing of another, while two covered their bodies. And each went straight forward; wherever the spirit would go, they went, without turning as they went. In the midst of the living creatures there was something that looked like burning coals of fire, like torches moving to and fro among the living creatures; and the fire was bright, and out of the fire went forth lightning. And the living creatures darted to and fro, like a flash of lightning.

Now as I looked at the living creatures, I saw a wheel upon the earth beside the living creatures, one for each of the four of them. As for the appearance of the wheels and their construction: their appearance was like the gleaming of a chrysolite; and the four had the same likeness, their construction being as it were a wheel within a wheel. When they went, they went in any of their four directions without turning as they went. The four wheels had rims and they had spokes; and their rims were full of eyes round about. And when the living creatures went, the wheels went beside them; and when the living creatures rose from the earth, the wheels rose. Wherever the spirit would go, they went, and the wheels rose along with them; for the spirit of the living creatures was in the wheels . . . Over the heads of the living creatures there was the likeness of a firmament, shining like crystal, spread out above their heads. And under the firmament their wings were stretched out straight, one toward another; and each creature had two wings covering its body. And when they went, I heard the sound of their wings like the sound of many waters, like the thunder of the Almighty, a sound of tumult like the sound of a host; when they stood still, they let down their wings. And there came a voice from above the firmament over their heads; when they stood still, they let down their wings.

And above the firmament over their heads there was the likeness of a throne, in appearance like sapphire, and seated above the likeness of a throne was a likeness as it were of a human form. And upwards from what had the appearance of his loins I saw as it were gleaming bronze, like the appearance of fire enclosed round about; and downwards from what had the appearance of his loins I saw as it were the appearance of fire, and there was brightness round about him. Like the appearance of the brightness round about. Such was the appearance of the likeness of the glory of the Lord. (Ezekiel 1:1–28)

Daniel's Dream Vision

The prophet Daniel lived at the beginning of the Hellenistic period – his prophecies were a series of visions about how those Jews who remained faithful to God during times of persecution would be delivered from their enemies. Here he has an awe-inspiring vision of a glorious figure.

On the twenty-fourth day of the first month, as I was standing on the bank of the great river, that is, the Tigris, I lifted up my eyes and looked, and behold a man clothed in linen, whose loins were girded with gold of Uphaz. His body was like beryl, his face like the appearance of lightning, his eyes like flaming torches, his arms and legs like the gleam of burnished bronze, and the sound of his words like the noise of a multitude. And I, Daniel, alone saw the vision, for the men who were with me did not see the vision, but a great trembling fell upon them, and they fled to hide themselves. So I was left alone and saw this great vision, and no strength was left in me, my radiant appearance was fearfully changed, and I retained no strength. Then I heard the sound of his words; and when I heard the sound of his words, I fell on my face in a deep sleep with my face to the ground.

And behold, a hand touched me and set me trembling on my hands and knees. And he said to me, 'O Daniel, man greatly beloved, give heed to the words that I speak to you, and stand upright, for now I have been sent to you.' While he was speaking this word to me, I stood up trembling. Then he said to me, 'Fear not, Daniel, for from the first day that you set your mind to understand and humbled yourself before your God, your words have been heard, and I have come because of your words. The prince came to make you understand what is to befall your people in the latter days. For the vision is for the days yet to come.' (Daniel 10:1–14)

PHILO AND DIVINE AGENCIES

According to rabbinic tradition, the spirit of prophecy departed from Israel after the death of the last post-exilic prophets. In the place of ecstatic experience, Jewish writers engaged in theological speculation about the nature of God and his relationship to the universe. Pre-eminent among Jewish thinkers of the Hellenistic period was Philo of Alexandria, who maintained that through divine agencies God was able to become immanent in the world. In On Dreams, *he described their activity.*

For God, not wishing to come down to the external senses, sends his own words [*logoi*] or angels in order to give assistance to those who love virtue. They attend like physicians to the diseases of the soul, apply themselves to heal them, offer sacred recommendations like sacred laws, and invite humans to practise the duties inculcated by them. Like the trainers of wrestlers, they implant in their pupils strength and power and irresistible vigour. Very properly, therefore, when he [Jacob] arrived at the external sense, he was represented no longer as meeting God, but only the divine word. (*On Dreams* 1.12)

PHILO'S INTERPRETATION OF GOD'S ACTION

For Philo angels are representatives of God among human beings. Using this theoretical framework, Philo expounded the meaning of Scripture where God is depicted as acting in the world. In Allegories of the Sacred Laws *he provided an account of Jacob's explanation of the relationship between God and the individual.*

These men pray to be nourished by the word [*logos*] of God. However Jacob, raising his head above the word, says that he is nourished by God himself. His words are as follows: 'The God in whom my father Abraham and Isaac were well pleased, the God who has nourished me from my youth to this day; the angel who delivered me from all my evils, bless these children.' Being a symbol of a perfect disposition, he now thinks God himself his nourisher, and not the word; he speaks of the angel, which is the word, as the physician of his evils, thereby speaking most naturally. The good things which he has previously mentioned are pleasing to him, inasmuch as the living and true God gave them to him face to face. However, the secondary good things have been given to him by the angels and by the word of God. On this account I think that God alone gives men pure good health which is not preceded by any disease in the body; but that health which is an escape from disease, he gives through the medium of skill and medical science. It is attributed to science and to whoever can apply it skilfully, even though in truth it is God himself who heals both by these means, and without these means. The same is the case with regard to the soul – the good things, namely, food, he gives to men by his power alone, but those which contain in them a deliverance from evil he gives by means of his angels and his word. (*Allegories of the Sacred Laws* 3.62)

PHILO AND THE ANGELIC REALM

In Philo's view, the angels as God's intermediaries occupy an angelic realm. Commenting on Genesis 28.12 ('And he [Jacob] dreamed a dream and behold a ladder was planted firmly on the ground, the head of which reached to heaven, and the angels of God were ascending and descending upon it'), he offered a description of this heavenly domain in On Dreams.

This air is the habitation of incorporeal souls because it seemed good to the Creator of the universe to fill all parts of the world with living creatures . . . The Creator of the universe formed the air so that it should be the dwelling place of those bodies which are immovable, the nature of those which are moved in an invisible manner, and the soul of those who are able to exert an impetus and visible sense of their own . . . As a result, let no one deprive the most excellent nature of living creatures of the most excellent of those elements which surround the earth; namely, the air. Not only is it not alone, deserted by all things besides; it is rather like a populous city, full of imperishable and immortal citizens, souls equal in number to the stars. Now, regarding these souls, some descend upon the earth so as to be bound up in mortal bodies . . . Others soar upwards . . . While others, condemning the body to be a great folly and trifling, have pronounced it a prison and a grave. Flying from it as from a house of correction or a tomb, they have raised themselves aloft on light

wings toward the aether, devoting their whole lives to sublime specu-
lations. Again there are others – the purest and most excellent of all
– who possess greater and more divine intellects and never by any
chance desire any earthly thing whatever. Being, as it were, lieuten-
ants of the Ruler of the universe, as though they were the eyes and
ears of the Great Kings, they behold and listen to everything.
Philosophers in general are apt to call these daemons, but the sacred
scriptures call them angels, using a name more in accord with nature.
(*On Dreams* 1.22)

METATRON

*Like Philo, rabbinic sages conceived of a divine messenger: Metatron.
In their view, Metatron acts as God's agency on earth; he is a link
uniting humanity with the Divine, pleads for Israel, and also takes on
himself the sorrow for Israel's sins as depicted in the* Introduction to
Lamentations Rabba.

No sooner had the Temple been burnt than the Holy One (blessed
be he) said, 'Now I shall withdraw my *Shekhinah* (Divine Presence)
from it and I shall go up to my former habitation as it is said. I will
go and return to my place, till they acknowledge their offence and
seek my face [Hosea 5.15]. At that time the Holy One (blessed be he)
wept, saying, 'Woe is me! What have I done! I caused my *Shekhinah*
to dwell below for the sake of Israel, but now that Israel has sinned
I have returned to my original dwelling place. Far be it from me that
I should become a source of derision to the nations and a mockery
to all creatures!' Immediately Metatron fell upon his face, exclaiming, 'O Sovereign of the universe, let me weep, but do not yourself
weep!' (*Introduction to Lamentations Rabba* 24)

WISDOM

*Like Metatron, divine wisdom was viewed as a link between God and
creation. Drawing on the notion of wisdom in Proverbs ('The Lord
possessed me in the beginning or ever the earth was' (Proverbs 8.22)),
Jewish writers of the second Temple period maintained that wisdom is
the attribute through which the Deity acts in the world. In the
Apocryphal* Wisdom of Solomon, *wisdom is presented as manifest in
all things.*

> For she is a breath of the power of God,
> And a clear effluence of the glory of the Almighty,

For she is an effluence from everlasting
And an unspotted mirror of the workin
(Wisdom of Solom

The *Shekhinah*

*For the rabbis God's presence in the universe wa_____
the* Shekhinah. *Based on such biblical passages as 'And let them make
me a sanctuary that I may dwell among them' (Exodus 15.8), rabbinic
sages maintained that the divine Spirit is continually in the midst of
Israel. As the* Mishnah *(second-century compilation of Jewish
law) 3.7 states:*

Rabbi Halafta, the son of Dosa, of the village of Hananya said,
'When ten people sit together and occupy themselves with the Torah,
the *Shekhinah* abides among them, as it is said, "God stands in the
congregation of the godly" [Psalms 82.1]. And whence can it be
shown that the same applies to five? Because it is said, "He has
founded his band upon the earth" [Amos 9.6]. And whence can it
be shown that the same applies to three. Because it is said, "He judges
among the judges" [Psalms 82.1]. And whence can it be shown that
the same applies to two? Because it is said, "Then they that feared
the Lord spake one with the other; and the Lord hearkened, and
heard" [Malachi 3.16]. And whence can it be shown that the same
applies even to one? Because it is said, "In every place where I cause
my name to be remembered, I will come unto you and I will bless
you." [Exodus 20.24]'

The Ten *Sefirot*

Pre-eminent among early mystical writings, the Sefer Yetsirah 1.4–14
(The Book of Creation) *provides a detailed explanation of the process
of creation. According to this anonymous work dating from the second
century* CE, *God created the universe through a process of emanation.
Like Philo and early rabbinic sages, the* Sefer Yetsirah *seeks to explain
how an infinite God could manifest himself in the universe. Drawing
on Neoplatonic ideas, it asserts that through ten* sefirot *(divine emanations) the cosmos was formed.*

There are ten intangible *sefirot*: ten and not nine; ten and not eleven.
Understand with wisdom, and be wise with understanding; test
them and explore them . . . Understand the matter fully, and set the
Creator in his place. Only he is the Former and Creator. There is

other. His attributes are ten and infinite. There are ten intangible *sefirot* whose measure is ten without end . . . Ten intangible
sefirot whose appearance is like lightning, whose limits are infinite.
His word is in them in their backward and forward movement, and
they run at his decree like the whirlwind, and they bow down before
his throne. There are ten intangible *sefirot* whose end is fixed in their
beginning, just as a flame is bound to coal.

One: spirit of living *Elohim* [God], blessed and blest is the name
of him who lives forever . . . His beginning has no beginning; his
end has no end.

Two: spiritual air from spirit. He engraved and hewed out in it
twenty-two letters as a foundation: three mothers, seven doubles,
and twelve simples. They are of one spirit.

Three: spiritual water from spiritual air. He engraved and hewed
out in it chaos and disorder, mud and mire. He engraved it like a
type of furrow. He raised it like a type of wall. He surrounded it like
a type of ceiling. He poured snow over them and it became earth,
as it is said, 'For he said to the snow, be earth' [Job 37.6].

Four: spiritual fire from spiritual water. He engraved and hewed
out in it the Throne of Glory, seraphim and *ophanim* (angels) and
hayyot [living creatures], and ministering angels. From the three of
them he established his dwelling place, as it is said, 'Who makes
winds his messengers, the flaming fire his ministers' [Psalms 104.4].

He chose three of the simple letters, sealed them with spirit and
set them into his great name, *YHV*, and sealed though them six
extremities. Five: he sealed height; he turned upwards and sealed it
with *YHV*. Six: he sealed abyss; he turned downwards, and sealed
it with *YHV*. Seven: he sealed east; he turned forwards and sealed it
with *HYV*. Eight: he sealed west; he turned backwards and sealed it
with *HYV*. Nine: he sealed south; he turned right and sealed it with
VYH. Ten: he sealed north; he turned left and sealed it with *VHY*.

These ten intangible *sefirot* are One – spirit of living *Elohim*;
spiritual air from spirit; spiritual water from spiritual air; spiritual
fire from spiritual water, height, abyss, east, west, north and south.

THE MOTHER LETTERS

In addition to the ten sefirot, *the* Sefer Yetsirah *3.2–10 depicts the
process of creation as taking place through the Hebrew letters. As the*
Sefer Yetsirah *relates, 'By means of the twenty-two letters, by giving
them a form and shape, by mixing them and combining them in different ways, God made the soul of all that which has been created and*

of all that which will be.' These twenty-two letters are divided into three groups, beginning with the three mother letters – aleph, mem, shin – which symbolize the elements air, fire and water.

Three mothers: *aleph, mem, shin.* A great secret, wonderful and hidden. He seals them with six rings. From them go out: air, fire and water. From them the fathers are born. From the Fathers, the progeny.

Three mothers: *aleph, mem, shin.* He engraved them. He hewed them. He combined them. He weighed them. He set them at opposites. He formed through them: three mothers – *aleph, mem, shin* in the universe; three mothers – *aleph, mem* and *shin* in the year; three mothers – *aleph, mem* and *shin* in the body of male and female.

Three mothers: *aleph, mem, shin.* The product of fire is heaven; the product of air is air; the product of water is earth. Fire is above; water is below; air tips the balance between them. From them, the fathers were generated, and from them, everything is created.

Three mothers: *aleph, mem, shin* are in the universe – air, water and fire. Heaven was created first from fire; earth from water; air from air.

Three mothers: *aleph, mem, shin* are in the year – cold, heat and temperate-state. Heat was created from fire; cold from water; temperate-state from air.

Three mothers: *aleph, mem, shin* are in the body of male and female – head, belly and chest. Head was created from fire; belly from water; chest from air.

He caused the letter *aleph* to reign over air . . . He combined them with one another. He formed through them: air in the universe, the temperate-state in the year, the chest in the body of male with *aleph, mem, shin,* and female with *aleph, mem, shin.*

He caused the letter *mem* to reign over water. He combined them with one another. He formed through them: earth in the universe; cold in the year; the belly in the body of male with *mem, aleph, shin,* and female with *shin, mem, aleph.*

He caused the letter *shin* to reign over fire. He combined them with one another. He formed through them: heaven in the universe; heat in the year; head in the body of male with *shin, aleph, mem,* and female with *shin, mem, aleph.*

THE SEVEN DOUBLE LETTERS

In addition to the mother letters, the Sefer Yetsirah 4.8 *asserts that seven double letters* (bet, gimel, dalet, kaf, pey, resh *and* tav) *were instrumental in the creation of the cosmos. These letters symbolize the contraries that exist in the universe.*

He caused the letter *bet* to reign over life . . . and he formed through them: Saturn in the universe, the first day in the year, and the right eye in the body of male and female.

He caused the letter *gimel* to reign over peace . . . He formed through them: Jupiter in the universe, the second day in the year, and the left eye in the body of male and female.

He caused the letter *dalet* to reign over wisdom . . . He formed through them: Mars in the universe, the third day in the year, and the left ear in the body of male and female.

He caused the letter *kaf* to reign over wealth . . . He formed through them: Sun in the universe, the fourth day in the year, and the left ear of the body of male and female.

He caused the letter *pey* to reign over gracefulness . . . He formed through them: Venus in the universe, the fifth day in the year, and the right nostril of the body of male and female.

He caused the letter *resh* to reign over seed . . . He formed through them: Mercury in the universe, the sixth day in the year, and the left nostril in the body of male and female.

He caused the letter *tav* to reign over dominion . . . He formed through them: Moon in the universe, the Sabbath day in the year, and the mouth in the body of male and female.

THE TWELVE SIMPLE LETTERS

In addition to the mother letters and the double letters, there are twelve simple letters (hey, vav, zayin, chet, tet, yod, lamed, nun, samech, ayin, tsade, kof), *which God utilized in creating the universe. These letters correspond to humans' chief activities – sight, hearing, smell, speech, desire for food, the sexual appetite, movement, anger, mirth, thought, sleep and work. In the* Sefer Yetsirah 5.3–5, *these letters are emblematic of the twelve signs of the zodiac in the heavenly sphere, the twelve months, and the chief limbs of the body. Thus, human beings, world and time are linked to one another through the process of creation.*

Twelve simple letters: *hey, vav, zayin, chet, tet, yod, lamed, nun, samech, ayin, tsade, kof.* He engraved their foundation, he hewed them out, he combined them, he weighed them, and he set them at opposites, and he formed through them: twelve constellations in the universe, twelve months in the year, twelve organs in the body of male and female.

The twelve constellations in the universe are: Aries, Taurus, Gemini, Cancer, Leo, Virgo, Libra, Scorpio, Sagittarius, Capricorn, Aquarius, Pisces.

The twelve months in the year are: *Nisan, Iyar, Sivan, Tammuz, Av, Elul, Tishri, Cheshvan, Kislev, Tevet, Shevat, Adar.*

The twelve organs in the body of male and female are: two hands, two feet, two kidneys, gall, small intestine, liver, gullet, stomach, spleen.

He caused the letter *hey* to reign over speech . . . He formed through them: Aries in the universe, and *Nisan* in the year, and the right foot in the body of male and female.

He caused the letter *vav* to reign over thought . . . He formed through them: Taurus in the universe, and *Iyar* in the year, and the right kidney in the body of male and female.

He caused the letter *zayin* to reign over movement . . . He formed through them: Gemini in the universe, and *Sivan* in the year, and the left foot in the body of male and female.

He caused the letter *chet* to reign over sight . . . He formed through them: Cancer in the universe, and *Tammuz* in the year, and the right hand in the body of male and female.

He caused the letter *tet* to reign over hearing . . . He formed through them: Leo in the universe, and *Av* in the year, and the left kidney in the body of male and female.

He caused the letter *yod* to reign over work . . . He formed through them: Virgo in the universe, and *Elul* in the year, and the left hand in the body of male and female.

He caused the letter *lamed* to reign over sexual intercourse . . . He formed through them: Libra in the universe, and *Tishri* in the year, and gall in the body of male and female.

He caused the letter *nun* to reign over smell . . . He formed through them: Scorpio in the universe, and *Cheshvan* in the year, and the small intestines in the body of male and female.

He caused the letter *samech* to reign over sleep . . . He formed through them: Sagittarius in the universe, and *Kislev* in the year, and the stomach in the body of male and female.

He caused the letter *ayin* to reign over wrath . . . He formed through them: Capricorn in the universe, and *Tevet* in the year, and the liver in the body of male and female.

He caused the letter *tsade* to reign over taste . . . He formed through them: Aquarius in the universe, and *Shevat* in the year, and the gullet in the body of male and female.

He caused the letter *kof* to reign over laughter . . . He formed through them: Pisces in the universe, and *Adar* in the year, and the spleen in the body of male and female.

A SECRET MYSTICAL QUEST

In these mystical reflections the first chapter of Ezekiel played a major role: here the merkavah *(divine chariot) is described in detail and this scriptural source served as a basis for speculation about the nature of the Deity. This mystical interpretation of the Bible was viewed as a secret quest, solely for the initiated. According to* Midrash Bereshit Rabbah *on Genesis 3, such interpretations should be repeated in a whisper so that no one else would hear them.*

Simeon, son of Jehozedek, asked Samuel, son of Nahman, and said to him, 'Seeing I have heard you are an expert in the *aggadah* [scriptural interpretation], tell me from where the light was created.' He replied that the *aggadah* tells us that the Holy One, blessed be he, wrapped himself in a garment and the brightness of his splendour lit up the universe. Samuel, son of Nahman, said this in a whisper, seeing that it is taught in Psalm 104.2, 'Who coverest thyself with light as with a garment.' 'Just as I myself had this whispered to me,' he said, 'even so have I whispered it to you.'

THE REQUIREMENTS FOR MYSTICAL STUDY

According to rabbinic tradition, only certain individuals should engage in mystical reflection – the insistence on moral and religious fitness was paramount. According to Talmud Kiddushin *71a, Judah said in the name of Rab (a third-century sage) that the use of God's name should be entrusted only to specific persons.*

The name of forty-two letters can only be entrusted by us to a person who is modest and meek, in the midway of life, not easily provoked to anger, temperate, and free from vengeful feelings. Whoever understands it, is cautious with it, keeps it in purity, is loved above and is liked here below. He is revered by his fellows; he is heir to two worlds – this world and the world to come.

THE DANGERS OF MYSTICAL REFLECTION

Without the correct attributes, those who sought to understand the divine mysteries could be in serious danger, as the sages in the Talmud explained in connection with a youth who sought to understand the nature of Ezekiel's vision of the merkavah.

A certain youth was once explaining the *hashmal* ['amber' in Ezekiel 1.27] when fire issued forth and consumed him.

MYSTICAL STUDY AND ALL-CONSUMING FIRE

For the rabbis the attainment of knowledge of the merkavah *was an exceedingly difficult task beset with obstacles.* Talmud Hagigah 2.1 *relates that even learned scholars were not immune from the hazards of fire.*

Johanan ben Zakkai was once riding on an ass, and Eliezer ben Arach was on an ass behind him. Eliezer ben Arach said to Johanan ben Zakkai, 'O master! Teach me a chapter of the *merkavah* mysteries.' 'No!' replied the master, 'Did I not already tell you that the *merkavah* may not be taught to anyone unless he is a sage and has an original turn of mind?' 'Very well, then!' replied Eliezer ben Arach. 'Will you give me permission to tell you a thing which you taught me?' 'Yes!' replied Johanan ben Zakkai, 'Say it!' Immediately the master dismounted from his donkey, wrapped himself in a garment, and sat on a stone beneath an olive tree. 'Why, O master, have you dismounted from your ass?' asked the disciple. 'Is it possible,' he replied, 'that I will ride on my donkey at the moment when you are expounding the mysteries of the *merkavah*, and the *Shekhinah* is with us, and the ministering angels are accompanying us?' Then Eliezer ben Arach began his discourse on the mysteries of the *merkavah*. No sooner had he begun, than fire came down from heaven and encompassed all the trees of the field, which with one accord, burst into song . . . An angel cried out from the fire, saying, 'Truly these, even these are the secrets of the *merkavah*.'

HEAVENLY ASCENT

According to rabbinic literature, certain pious individuals were able to ascend the heavenly heights through mystical reflection. After living spiritual lives, these sages were able to attain a state of ecstasy and behold visions as well as voices that brought them into contact with the

Divine. Yet Talmud Hagigah *14b relates that such mystical ascent was dangerous, even for such as Ben Azzai, Ben Zoma, Akiva and Aher. Ben Azzai died because he was overpowered by the experience; Ben Zoma was stricken when he gazed at the* merkavah, *and Aher became a dualist. Only Akiva was able to return unharmed.*

Our rabbis taught that four entered an orchard. These are they: Ben Azzai, Ben Zoma, Aher and Akiva. Akiva said to them, 'When you reach the stones of pure marble, do not say, "Water, water!" For it is said, "He who speaks falsehood shall not be established before my eyes."' Ben Azzai gazed and died. Concerning him Scripture says, 'Precious in the sight of the Lord is the death of his saints.' Ben Zoma gazed and was stricken. Concerning him Scripture says, 'Have you found honey? Eat as much as is sufficient for you, lest you be filled therewith, and vomit it.' Aher cut down the shoots. Akiva departed in peace.

The Seven Heavens

Early rabbinic scholars attempted to gaze at the merkavah *and the heavenly halls through an ascent of the soul. Such a tradition dates back to the apocalypticists who sought to uncover the future outcome of events that would take place at the end of time. Those who strove to make this ascent were referred to as the 'Riders of the Chariot'. Descriptions of the seven heavens and the angelic hosts were an important feature of the Talmud.*

The distance from the earth to the firmament is a journey of five hundred years . . . Above them are *hayyot* [the living creatures]. The feet of the holy are equal to all of them together. The ankles of the holy are equal to all of them. The legs of the holy are equal to all of them. The knees of the holy are equal to all of them. The thighs of the holy are equal to all of them. The bodies of the holy are equal to all of them. The necks of the holy are equal to all of them. The heads of the holy are equal to all of them. The horns of the holy are equal to all of them. Above them is the Throne of Glory. The feet of the Throne are equal to all of them. The Throne of Glory is equal to all of them. The King, the living and eternal God, high and exalted, dwells above them.

Ezekiel and the Heavenly Halls

The earliest hekhalot *(heavenly hall) source describing the heavenly halls dates from the fourth or fifth century and is a commentary on the first verse of the book of Ezekiel ('In the thirteenth year, in the fourth month, on the fifth day of the month, as I was among the exiles by the river Chebar, the heavens were opened, and I saw visions of God'). This early* midrash, The Vision of Ezekiel, *is typical of the* merkavah *mystics. Concerning the phrase, 'I was among the exiles by the river Chebar,' Rabbi Judah Ha-Nasi explained the nature of Ezekiel's complaint.*

Ezekiel began to complain to the Holy One, blessed be he, saying, 'Sovereign of the universe! Am I not a priest and a prophet? Why did Isaiah prophesy in Jerusalem yet I have to prophesy among the captives? Why did Hosea prophesy in Jerusalem, yet I have to prophesy among the captives? Of Isaiah it is written, "The vision of Isaiah." If it is because their prophecies brought good tidings and mine evil, it is not so, rather mine are good and theirs were evil.' A parable was told. To what can this be compared? To a king of flesh and blood with many servants to whom he allotted tasks to perform. He made the cleverest a shepherd, whereupon that clever man protested, 'My colleagues stay in an inhabited place; why should I have to be in the wilderness?' Similarly, Ezekiel protested, 'All my colleagues were in Jerusalem, why should I have to be among the captives?' No sooner did Ezekiel speak in this fashion than the Holy One, blessed be he, opened seven compartments down below. These are the compartments down below. Ezekiel gazed into these in order to see all that is on high.

THE REFLECTION OF THE SEVEN HEAVENS

According to The Vision of Ezekiel, *as Ezekiel gazed, God opened the seven heavens to him and he saw the* merkavah. *This was compared to a parable about a person who visited his barber.*

After the barber cut his hair, he gave him a mirror in which to look. As he was looking into the mirror the king passed by; he saw the king and his armies passing by the door [reflected in the mirror]. The barber said to him, 'Look behind you and you will see the king.' The man replied, 'I have already seen.' Thus Ezekiel stood beside the river Chebar gazing into the water and the seven heavens were opened to him so that he saw the glory of the Holy One, blessed be he, the *hayyot*, the ministering angels, the angelic hosts, the seraphim, those of sparkling wings, all attached to the *merkavah*. They passed by in heaven while Ezekiel saw them reflected in the water. For this reason the verse says 'by the river Chebar'.

SEVEN HEAVENS

The Vision of Ezekiel *asks why the biblical text refers to 'heaven' in the plural. The reason is because seven heavens were opened to Ezekiel.*

This teaches that seven heavens were opened to Ezekiel: *Shamayyim* [Heaven]; *Shemei ha-Shamayyim* [Heaven of Heavens]; *Zevul* [Fourth Heaven]; *Araphel* [Darkness]; *Shehakim* [Skies]; *Aravot* [Seventh Heaven], and the Throne of Glory.

SHAMAYYIM

Commenting on the nature of the seven heavens, The Vision of Ezekiel *declares that it is a five-hundred-year journey from the earth to the firmament.*

Rabbi Isaac said, 'It is a five-hundred-year journey from the earth to the firmament, as it is said, "That your days may be multiplied, and the days of your children . . . as the days of the heaven upon the earth" [Deuteronomy 11.21]. The thickness of the firmament is a five-hundred-year journey. The firmament contains only the sun, moon and stars but there is one *merkavah* therein. What is the name of this *merkavah*? It is *Rekhesh* [swift steed], as it is said, "Bind the chariot [*ha-merkavah*] to the swift steed [*Rekhesh*]" [Micah 1.13]. The waters above the firmament are a five-hundred-year journey, as it is said, "And God called the firmament heaven [*Shamayyim*]." Read not *Shamayyim* but *Sham Mayyim* [Water is there]. How is it formed? It is like a tent, as it is said, "It is he that sitteth above the circle of the earth . . . And spreadeth them out as a tent to dwell in." It is fashioned in no other way than as a dome. It is thicker than the earth; its edges reach to the sea and the wind enters in at the sides in order to divide the upper waters from the lower waters.

SHEMEI HA-SHAMAYYIM

The Vision of Ezekiel *states that it is a five-hundred-year journey from the sea to the* Shemei ha-Shamayyim *where the angels who say the* kedushah *(holiness prayer) are located. According to Rabbi Levi, they are renewed daily.*

They are not there permanently but, as Rabbi Levi said, 'They are new every morning, [Lamentations 3.23]. Rabbi Judah Ha-Nasi said, 'From where are they created? From *nehar di-nur* [river of fire].' No sooner have they been created than they stretch out their hands to take the fire of *nehar di-nur* with which they wash their lips and tongues before reciting the *kedushah*.

Their voices continue unceasingly from sunrise to sunset, as it is said, 'From the rising of the sun unto the going down thereof the Lord's name is praised' [Psalms 113.3]. Then they are hidden away and others created to take their place. Therein is the *merkavah*. What is the name of this *merkavah*? It is *Susim* [horses], as it is said, 'I saw in the night, and behold a man riding upon a red horse' (Zechariah 1.3).

FROM *SHEMEI HA-SHAMAYYIM* TO *ZEVUL*

The Vision of Ezekiel asserts that it is a five-hundred-year journey from Shemei ha-Shamayyim *to* Zevul. *In answer to the question of what is in* Zevul, *Rabbi Levi said in the name of Rabbi Hama bar Ukba and in the name of Rabbi Johanan:*

The Prince is in no other place than in *Zevul*. He is the very fullness of *Zevul* and before him there are thousands and myriads of myriads who minister before him. Concerning them Daniel says, 'I behold till thrones were placed ... A fiery stream ... Thousand thousands ministered unto him' [Daniel 9–10]. What is his name? It is *Kimos*. Rabbi Isaac said, '*Meattah* is his name.' Rabbi Inyanei bar Sisson said, '*Bi-Zevul* is his name.' Rabbi Tanhum the Elder said, '*Atatiya* is his name.' Eleazar Nadvadaya said, 'Metatron, like the name of the Power.' And those who make theurgical use of the divine name say, '*Sanas* is his name; *Kas, Bas, Bas, Kevas* is his name, like the name of the Creator of the world.' And what is the name, of the *merkavah* that is in *Zevul*? *Halvayah* is its name concerning which David said, 'To him that rideth upon the heaven of heavens' (Psalms 66.34).

FROM *ZEVUL* TO *ARAPHEL*

According to the Vision of Ezekiel, *from* Zevul *to* Araphel *is again a five-hundred-year journey, and the thickness of this heaven is similarly a five-hundred-year journey.* The Vision of Ezekiel *describes its interior.*

Therein is the canopy of the Torah, as it is said, 'But Moses drew near unto the thick darkness [*Araphel*] where God was' [Exodus 20.18]. There is the *merkavah* upon which the Holy One, blessed be he, descended upon Mount Sinai. What is its name? It is the chariot of kings, concerning which David said, 'The chariots of God are myriads even thousands upon thousands; the Lord is among them, as in Sinai, in holiness' [Psalms 68.18].

From *Araphel* to *Shehakim*

This depiction of the seven heavens continues in Vision of Ezekiel, *describing the distance between* Araphel *and* Shehakim *and its contents.*

From *Araphel* to *Shehakim* is a five-hundred-year journey; the thickness thereof is a five-hundred-year journey. What is therein? The rebuilt Jerusalem, the Temple and the Sanctuary, the Testimony, the Ark, the *Menorah* [candelabrum], the Table, the sacred vessels and all the adornments of the Temple together with the *manna* that was eaten by the Israelites. How do we know that all the sacred vessels are there? For it is said, 'Ascribe ye strength unto God . . . and his strength is in the skies' (Psalms 68.35). Therein is a *merkavah*. What is the name of this *merkavah*? It is cherubim, upon which he rode when he went down to the sea, as it is said, 'And he rode upon a cherub, and did fly' (Psalms 18.11).

From *Shehakim* to *Aravot*

From Shehakim *to* Aravot *involves first a five-hundred-year journey to* Makhon. The Vision of Ezekiel *maintains that in its midst are the storehouses of snow and of hail, as well as dreadful punishments reserved for the wicked and rewards for the righteous. Then from* Makhon *to* Aravot *is another five-hundred-year journey.*

The thickness thereof is a five-hundred-year journey. What is therein? The treasures of blessing, the storehouses of snow, the storehouses of peace, the souls of the righteous and the souls yet to be born, the dreadful punishments reserved for the wicked and the rewards for the righteous. What is the name of the *merkavah* that is there? *Av* [cloud] is its name, as it is said, 'The burden of Egypt. Behold, the Lord rideth upon a swift cloud' (Isaiah 19.1).

From *Aravot* to the Throne of Glory

According to the Vision of Ezekiel, *it is a five-hundred-year journey from* Aravot *to the Throne of Glory and its thickness is also a five-hundred-year journey.*

What is therein? The hooves of the *hayyot* [living creatures] and part of the wings of the *hayyot*, as it is said, 'And under the firmament were their wings conformable.' Therein is a great chariot on which the Holy One, blessed be he, will descend in the future to judge all the nations, concerning which Isaiah said, 'For behold, the Lord will come in fire, and his chariots shall be like the whirlwind' (Isaiah 66.15). What is its name? It is Chariots of Fire and Whirlwind.

HEKHALOT RABBATI

Another early hekhalot text, Hekhalot Rabbati (The Greater Heavenly Halls), contains a detailed explanation of the experiences of the Riders of the Chariot.

When one is on a higher level, he can enter. He is brought in and led to the heavenly chambers where he is permitted to stand before the Throne of Glory. He then knows what will happen in the future, who will be raised up, who will be lowered, who will be made strong, who will be cut off, who will be made poor, who will be made rich, who will die, who will live, who will have his inheritance taken away from him, who will have it given to him, who will be invested with the Torah, and who will be given wisdom. When one is on a higher level, he can see all the secret deeds of man ... When one is on a higher level, he knows all kinds of sorcery ... When one is on a higher level, whoever speaks against him maliciously is taken and cast down ... When one is on a higher level, he is separated from all men, and distinguished from all humanity by his traits. He is honoured by those on earth and by those on high.

RABBI NEHUNYA BEN HAKKANAH AND THE DIVINE CHARIOT

The historical setting of Rabbi Nehunya ben Hakkanah's discourse was the Roman persecution of the Jews in the years 120–35. Chapter 15 of Hekhalot Rabbati sets the stage for later revelations.

Rabbi Ishmael said that when Rabbi Nehunya ben Hakkanah saw that Rome was planning to destroy the mighty of Israel, he immediately revealed the secret of the world as it appears to the person who is worthy to gaze on the King and his Throne in his majesty and his beauty – on the *hayyot* of holiness, the cherubim of might, and the wheels of the *Shekhinah*, which are as lightning mixed with awesome electrum, on the beauty which is around the Throne, on the bridges and the growing chains which rise between the bridges, on the dust, smoke, and the wind which raises the dust of the coals for it conceals and covers all the chambers of the place of *Aravot-Rakia* with the clouds of its coals, and on *Surya*, the Prince of the Presence, the servant of *Totarkhiel-YHVH*, the proud one.

THE SCHOLARS AND THE DIVINE CHARIOT

Chapter 16 of Hekhalot Rabbati *depicts the gathering of scholars at the place where the third gate of the Temple stood; there Rabbi Nehunya ben Hakkanah discoursed on the* merkavah.

Rabbi Ishmael said, 'I stood and gathered the whole Great Tribunal and the Lesser Tribunal, bringing them to the third great hall of the House of God ... Those who came included Rabbi Shimon ben Gamaliel, Rabbi Eliezer the Great, Rabbi Elazar ben Dama, Rabbi Eliezer ben Shamua, Rabbi Yochanan ben Dahavai, Rabbi Chananya ben Chanikai, Rabbi Jonathan ben Uziel, Rabbi Akiva and Rabbi Yehuda ben Bava. We all came and sat before [Rabbi Nehunya ben Hakkanah]. The throngs of our companions stood, for they saw rivers of fire and brilliant flames separating them from us. Rabbi Nehunya ben Hakkanah sat and explained everything about the *merkavah*. He described its descent and ascent; how one who descends must descend, and how one who ascends must ascend. When a person wishes to descend to the *merkavah*, he must call upon *Surayah*, the Prince of the Face. He must then bind him by an oath 112 times, in the name of *Tutrsyay*, the Lord who is called: *Tutrsyay Tzurtk Tutrbyal, Tofgr Ashruylyay Zvudial*, and *Zhrryal Tndal Shudk, Yozya Dhyvuryn* and *Adiryron* – the Lord, God of Israel. One should not add to these 112 times, nor should he subtract from them. For if one adds or subtracts, his blood is on his head. His mouth should utter the names, and with his fingers, he should count up to 112. He then immediately descends and has authority over the *merkavah*.

THE ANGELIC REALM

According to Chapter 17 of the Hekhalot Rabbati, *angels guard the heavenly heights.*

Rabbi Ishmael said, 'Thus said Rabbi Nehunya ben Hakkanah, "*Titrsyay*, the Lord, God of Israel dwells in seven chambers, one within the other. At the door of each chamber are eight gatekeepers, four to the right of the lintel; four to the left. These are the names of the watchers at the door of the first chamber: *Dahaviel, Kashriel,*

Gahuriel, Buthiel, Tofhiel, Dahariel, Mathkiel and *Shaviel*. These are the names of the watchers at the door of the second chamber: *Tagriel, Mathpiel, Sarchiel, Arpiel, Shaharariel, Satriel, Ragaiel* and *Sahiviel*. These are the names of the watchers at the door of the third chamber: *Shaburiel, Ratzutziel, Shalmiel, Sabliel, Zachzachiel, Hadariel* and *Bazriel*. These are the names of the watchers at the door of the fourth chamber: *Pachadiel, Geburathiel, Cazviel, Shekhinyael, Shathakiel, Araviel, Capiel* and *Anpiel*. These are the names of the watchers at the door of the fifth chamber: *Techiel, Uziel, Gatiel, Gatchiel, Saafriel, Garfiel, Gariel, Dariel* and *Paltriel*. These are the names of the watchers at the door of the sixth chamber: *Dumiel, Katzpiel, Gahagahiel, Arsbarsabiel, Agromiel, Partziel, Machakiel* and *Tofriel*. At the door of the seventh chamber stand all the mighty ones, terrifying, powerful, fearsome ... They bear sharp swords in their hands, flashing lightning rays from their eyes, streams of fire from their nostrils, burning coals from their mouths. They are adorned with helmet and armour, with spears and lances hanging at their sides."

Descent to the *Merkavah*

According to Chapter 18 of Hekhalot Rabbati, *those who descend to the* merkavah *are not harmed, even though they are able to see the palaces of the higher realm.*

All those who go to the *merkavah* are not injured even though they are able to see all the palaces. They descend in peace, returning and testifying to the awesome, terrifying sight they have perceived, the like of which cannot be experienced in any of the palaces of flesh and blood. In consequence they bless, praise, extol, exalt, laud and give glory, tribute and greatness to *Tutrsyay-YHVY*, Lord of Israel, who rejoices with those who descend to the *merkavah*. He sits and waits for each Israelite when he comes down in wondrous proudness and in strange powerfulness, a proudness of exultation and the powerfulness of radiance as these are aroused before the Throne of Glory three times daily, in heaven, from creation until now to sing his praise.

Passage Through the Palaces

Hekhalot Rabbati *provides instructions for passage through the gates of the palaces. According to Chapter 19, as one advances through the first five palaces, he should show a seal from* YHVH *(Lord of Israel) to* the guards on the right, and a seal from Metatron to the guards on the left. Here are recorded various mysterious names of those present in the heavenly heights.

Rabbi Ishmael said, 'When you come to the door of the first chamber, take two seals in your hand, one of *Tutrosyay*, the Lord, and one of *Surayah*, Prince of the Face. That of *Tutrosyay* show to those standing on the right, and that of *Surayah*, show to those on the left. *Dahaviel*, the angel who is the chief guardian of the door of the first chamber and overseer of the first chamber, who stands at the right of the lintel, and *Tofhiel*, the angel who stands at the left of the lintel with him, will immediately grasp you. They will give you to *Tagriel*, the angel who is the chief guardian of the door of the second chamber, who stands to the right of the lintel, and to *Mathpiel*, the angel who stands with him to the left of the lintel. Show them two seals, one of *Adryhron*, the Lord, and one of *Ohazyya*, the Prince of the Face. That of *Adryhron* show to those who stand at the right, and of *Ohazyya*, Prince of the Face, show to those who stand at the left. Immediately they will grasp you, one to the right and one to the left. Perfecting and illuminating you, they will turn you over to *Shaburiel*, the angel who is the chief guardian of the third chamber, who stands to the left of the lintel, and to *Ratzutziel*, the angel who stands with him to the left. Show them two seals, one of *Tzurtk* the Lord, and one of *Dahavyoron*, the Prince of the Face. That of *Tzurtk*, the Lord, show to those who stand to the right, and that of *Dahavyoron*, Prince of the Face, to those who stand to the left. Immediately they will grasp you, one to your right and one to your left, and two angels will precede you and two will follow you. Perfecting and illuminating you, they will bring you to *Pachadiel*, the chief guardian of the door of the fourth chamber, standing at the right of the lintel, and to *Geburathiel*, the angel who stands to the left of the lintel with him. Show them two seals, one of *Zvudiel*, the Lord, and one of *Margiviel*, Prince of the Face. That of *Zvudiel*, show to those who stand to the right, and that of *Margiviel*, Prince of the Face, show to those who stand on the left. Immediately, they will grasp you, one to the right and one to the left. Perfecting and illuminating you, they will turn you over to *Techiel*, the angel who is head of the fifth chamber, who stands to the right of the lintel, and to *Uziel*, the angel who stands to the left of the lintel with him. Show them two seals, one of *Tutrbyal*, the Lord, and one of *Zachapniryai*, Prince of the Face. That of *Tutrbyal* show to those standing at the right, and that of *Zachapniryai*, Prince of the Face, show to those standing to the left. Immediately angels will grasp you, three from the front, and three from behind.

THE DANGERS OF THE SIXTH PALACE

According to Chapter 19 of Hekhalot Rabbati, grave hazards are associated with mystical ascent (here referred to as a descent to the merkavah).

The guards of the sixth palace make a practice of attacking those who descend and do not descend into the *merkavah* without authority. They throng around such individuals, striking them and burning them. They then send others in their places who do the same. They have no compunction, nor do they ever stop to ask, 'Why are we burning them? What enjoyment do we have when we assail those individuals who descend to the *merkavah* and do not descend without authority?' This is the trait of the guardians at the door of the sixth chamber.

RABBI NEHUNYA BEN HAKKANAH'S VISION

Troubled by Nahunya's discourse, the sages asked Rabbi Ishmael to bring him back from his vision of the merkavah *so that he would be able to relate what he had experienced. Thus Chapter 20 of* Hekhalot Rabbati *relates:*

Rabbi Ishmael said, 'The members of the group said to me, "Son of the proud, you rule through the light of the Torah, just like Rabbi Nehunya ben Hakkanah. See if you can bring him back from his vision. Let him sit with us and explain the meaning of those who 'descend to the *merkavah* but do not descend'. Why are they attacked by the guardians of the sixth chamber? Why do they not touch those who descend into the *merkavah*? What is the difference between the two?"' Rabbi Ishmael replied, 'I immediately took a cloth of feathery down and gave it to Rabbi Akiva. Rabbi Akiva gave it to our servant, telling him to touch it to a woman who had immersed in the *mikveh* [ritual bath] incorrectly.' This was to be a case such that if brought to the sages, she would have been viewed as forbidden, even though the majority would say that she was permitted . . . They did this, and placed the cloth before Rabbi Ishmael. He took it on a perfumed twig of myrtle which had been soaked in pure balsam. He then placed it on the knees of Rabbi Nehunya ben Hakkanah, who was immediately dismissed from before the Throne of Glory . . . We then asked him, 'Who are the ones who descend into the *merkavah*, but do not descend into the *merkavah*?' He said, 'These are individuals taken along by those who descend into the *merkavah*. Their guides stand them above their heads, and place them in front of them, saying, "Gaze, look and listen, and write all that I say, and all that we hear from before the Throne of Glory." These people are not worthy of this and in consequence are attacked by the guardians of the sixth chamber. You should therefore be careful that you select proper individuals; they should be members of the society who have been screened.'

REQUIREMENTS FOR DESCENT

Chapter 21 of The Hekhalot Rabbati *discusses the requirements for descent to the* merkavah.

At the right of the door of the sixth palace is the angel *Dumiel*, keeper of the gate, to the right of the door. He sits on a couch of pure platinum, glowing like the radiance of the heavens, like the covenant of the universe. *Arstan, Myra Arstan* and *Cnpynn Tzmnsh Ernh*, the Lord, God of Israel, and the angel *Dumiel* receive an individual with pleasant countenance, sitting him on a couch of pure platinum. They then sit by him to his right. He says to him, 'I bear witness concerning two things and warn you. One should not descend to the *merkavah* unless he possesses two qualifications. First, he must have read and reviewed the Torah, prophets and writings, and have mastered the *Mishnah* [the Law], and the *aggadah* [rabbinic commentary], as well as the deeper meaning of law regarding what is permitted and what forbidden. Secondly, he must be an individual who keeps the entire Torah, and heeds all its prohibitions, decrees, judgements and laws taught to Moses on Mount Sinai.'

THE PASSAGE OF THE INITIATE

The Hekhalot Rabbati *continues to describe the descent of the initiate to the* merkavah. *According to Chapter 22, once an individual has passed the test of the sixth palace, he is able to continue his journey through the heavenly realm.*

If a person has these two qualifications, then the angel *Dumiel* entrusts him to Gabriel the scribe. He then writes a note with red ink and hangs it on the chariot of that individual. The note describes the initiate's Torah scholarship as well as his deeds, and states that he wishes to come before the Throne of Glory. When the guardians of the door of the seventh palace see *Dumiel*, *Gabriel* and *Katzpiel* coming before the chariot of the individual worthy of descending to the *merkavah*, they cover their faces, and since they were previously standing they sit down. They also unloosen their drawn bows and return their swords to their sheaths. Even so one must continue to show them the great seal and fearsome crown of *Aer Sobr Mtzugyyh* and *Beshptsh* the Lord, God of Israel. They then bring him before the Throne of Glory. They take out all kinds of musical instruments and play before him until they elevate him and sit him next to the cherubim next to the ophanim, and next to the holy *hayyot*. He then sees wonders and powers, majesty and greatness, holiness, purity, terror, humility and uprightness.

The Names of the Guards of the Seventh Palace

In Chapter 23 of The Hekhalot Rabbati *the names of the guardians of the seventh palace are listed.*

'Concerning the guards of the gates of the six palaces, one has authority to mention the names of God and to use them, but as for the guards of the gates of the seventh palace, the very hearing of these names causes a person to be thrown into panic as how to use them since the name of every one of them is derived from the name of the King of the universe, and I have not specified them. Now that you say to me, "Specify them", come stand every one of you. When the name of each comes forth from your mouth, bow down and fall on your faces.' Immediately all the mighty men of the group came and all the mighty of the *yeshivah* stood on their feet before Rabbi Nehunya ben Hakkanah . . . These are the names of the guardians of the seventh palace specified by ascent: *Zehpanuryay YVY*, an honoured and beloved angel, *Abirzehyay YVY*, an honoured, beloved and fearsome angel. *Atarigiash YVY*, an honoured, beloved, fearsome and astounding angel. *Nagarniel YVY*, an honoured, beloved, fearsome, astounding and precious angel. *Anpiel YVY*, an honoured, beloved, fearsome, astounding, precious and exalted angel. *Naazuriel YVY*, an honoured, beloved, fearsome, astounding, precious, exalted and mighty angel. *Sastiel YVY*, an honoured, beloved, fearsome, astounding, precious, exalted, mighty and majestic angel. *Anpiel YVY*, an angel whose name is uttered before the Throne of Glory three times each day . . . These are the names of the guardians of the seventh palace specified by the descent: *Nurpiel YVY*, an honoured, beloved, fearsome angel, who is called *Abirhyay YVY*. *Dalukiel YVY*, an honoured, beloved and fearsome angel, who is called *Levkapiel YVY*. *Yakriel YVY*, an honoured, beloved and fearsome angel, who is

called *Atrigiel YVY. Yasisiel YVY*, an honoured, beloved and fearsome angel, who is called *Banaaniel YVY. Nurpiniel YVY*, an honoured, beloved and fearsome angel, who is called *Shakadyahiel YVY.
Naarukriel YVY*, an honoured, beloved and fearsome angel, who is
called *Zuhaliel YVY. Anpiel YVY*, an honoured, beloved, fearsome,
astounding, precious, exalted, mighty, majestic, powerful, upright
and stupendous angel, who is called *Tufriel YVY.*

THE FOUR *HAYYOT*

When the gates to the seventh palace are opened, the four hayyot
described by Ezekiel appear. Chapter 24 of Hekhalot Rabbati *describes
their nature.*

As soon as that person entreats to descend to the *merkavah, Anpiel*,
the Prince, opens the doors of the seventh palace and that individual
enters and stands on the threshold of the gate of the seventh palace.
The holy *hayyot* lift him up. Five hundred and twelve eyes, and each
and every eye of the eyes of the holy *hayyot* is hollow like the holes
in a sieve woven of branches. These eyes appear like lightning, and
they dart to and fro. In addition, there are the eyes of the cherubim
of might and the wheels of the *Shekhinah*, which are like torches of
light and flames of burning coals. This person then trembles, shakes,
moves to and fro, panics, is terrified, faints and collapses backwards.
Anpiel, the Prince, and sixty-three watchmen of the seven gates of
the palace support him, and they all help him and say, 'Do not fear,
son of the beloved seed. Enter and see the King in his magnificence.
You will not be slaughtered and you will not be burnt.'

BEFORE THE THRONE OF GLORY

Chapter 25 of The Hekhalot Rabbati *explains that when a person
stands before the Throne of Glory, he begins to chant a hymn of
glory:*

> King of the King of Kings, God of Gods, and Lord of
>   Lords,
> Who is surrounded with chains of crowns,
> Who is encompassed by the cluster of the rulers of
>   radiance,
> Who covers the heavens with the wing of his
>   magnificence,
> And in his majesty appeared from the heights,

From his beauty the deeps are kindled,
And from his stature the heavens are sparked.
His stature sends out the lofty,
And his crown blazes out the might,
And his garment flows with the precious.
And all trees shall rejoice in his word,
And herbs shall exult in his rejoicing,
And his words shall drop as perfumes,
Flowing forth in flames of fire,
Giving joy to those who search them,
And quiet to those who fulfil them.

2 Medieval Jewish Mysticism
c.900–c.1300

Introduction

In the early medieval period the mystical texts of rabbinic Judaism were studied by scholars living in the Rhineland. Among the greatest figures of this period were the twelfth-century Samuel ben Kalonymus of Speyer, his son Judah ben Samuel of Regensburg, who wrote the *Sefer Hasidim* (*The Book of the Pious*), and Eleazar ben Judah of Worms, who composed the treatise *The Secret of Secrets*. In their writings these mystics were preoccupied with the mystery of divine unity. In the formulation of their theological doctrines the *Hasidei Ashkenaz* (Pious of Germany) engaged in the study of the names of God and the mystical combination of the letters of these names. Within this theological framework the concept of the *hasid* (pious person) was of paramount importance; to be a *hasid* was a religious ideal that transcended all intellectual accomplishments. Eleazar ben Judah's *The Secret of Secrets* described such a life of piety.

Another feature of this movement concerned prayer mysticism. In the literature of the pietists, attention was given to techniques of mystical speculation based on the calculation of the words in prayers, benedictions and hymns. Parallel with these developments, Jewish mystics in southern France engaged in mystical speculation about the nature of God, the soul, the existence of evil and the religious life. In twelfth-century Provence the earliest kabbalistic text, the *Bahir* (*The Book of Light*), reinterpreted the concept of the *sefirot* (divine emanations) as depicted in the *Sefer Yetsirah* (*The Book of Creation*). Basing themselves on this anonymous work, various Jewish sages of Provence engaged in similar mystical reflection. Isaac the Blind, for example, conceived of the *sefirot* as emanations of a hidden dimension of the Godhead. In Gerona his teachings were broadly disseminated, influencing such figures as Azriel of Gerona, who, in the *Gate of Kavvanah* (*The Gate of Intention*), formulated a theory of mysticism of light, related to the *sefirot*.

During the time that these Geronese mystics were propounding their kabbalistic theories, different mystical schools of thought developed in other parts of Spain. Influenced by the *Hasidei Ashkenaz* and the Súfí traditions of Islam, Abraham ben Samuel Abulafia advanced techniques of letter manipulation as a means of attaining prophecy. Other kabbalistic figures of this period, such as Joseph Gikatilla and Isaac of Acco, were similarly preoccupied with the technique of letter manipulation. A different approach to divine illumination was advanced during this period by Jacob of Marvège in his *Responsa from Heaven*, in which he submitted questions to God by using various combinations of the divine name. Eventually the mingling of gnostic teaching with the *kabbalah* (mystical tradition) of Gerona resulted in the publication of the most important mystical work of Spanish Jewry, the *Zohar* (*The Book of Splendour*), composed by Moses ben Shem Tov de Leon in Guadalajara.

The Life of Piety

The mystical texts of early rabbinic Judaism were studied by Jewish settlers in the Rhineland from approximately the ninth century. During the twelfth and thirteenth centuries these authorities – the Hasidei Ashkenaz – delved into the Sefer Yetsirah and hekhalot (heavenly hall) literature. Among the greatest figures of this period was Eleazar ben Judah of Worms, who described the fear and love of God in his The Secret of Secrets (part of which was incorporated into a later mystical collection, The Book of Raziel). In his view, the life of piety is a necessary stage in the quest for divine enlightenment through the study of the merkavah (divine chariot).

'Let a man always be subtle in the fear of God.' This means that a person should reflect on the subtleties and the glories of the world: how, for example, a mortal king commands his soldiers to engage in battle. Even though they know they may be killed, they are afraid of him and obey him even though they know that the fear of him is not everlasting, because he will eventually die and perish and they can escape to another country. How much more so, therefore, should men fear the King of the King of Kings, the Holy One, blessed be he, and walk in his ways, since he is everywhere and gazes at the wicked as well as the good.

The Root of the Fear of God

In The Secret of Secrets *Eleazar ben Judah explained that the root of the fear of God is when people desire something and yet give up the pleasure for which they crave because they fear God.*

It is not that he fears punishment in this world or in the next but rather he is afraid that he may not be perfect before God whom he loves. When a good deed presents itself to him and he finds it very difficult to perform, he nonetheless performs it, just as Abraham did when he bound his son on the altar, as it is written, 'For now I know that you are a God-fearing man' [Genesis 22.12].

'Now I know?' Surely, he knew it before the world was created, as it is said, 'Before I formed you in the belly I knew you' [Jeremiah 1.5]. Yet the meaning is, 'I shall not test you any further. Since you have done this thing it is obvious that your heart is whole in all which I command you. I do not have to test you any more since if you were ready to do this, everything else is included.'

This has to be understood on the basis of the verse, 'Now I know that the Lord is greater than all gods' [Exodus 18.11], that there is no longer any need to try any other gods. And Joseph said, 'For I fear God' [Genesis 42.18]. It is difficult for me to send you away since you are spies but I fear God who does not want your children to go hungry. And Obadiah 'feared the Lord greatly' [1 Kings 18.3], because he found it a very difficult thing to do, for if Jezebel heard of it she would have had him killed.

But when it says, 'You shall fear your God' [Leviticus 19.14], it refers to something in the heart. And when it says, 'You shall fear the Lord your God' [Deuteronomy 10.20], and 'O fear the Lord, you his holy ones' [Psalms 34.10], it refers to things very hard for the heart to bear – they present a challenge to the fear of God.

Abraham had feared God because he imagined that if he did not take Isaac, God would then kill him, which would have been a hard thing to do. But here Abraham is prepared to kill himself. This was the most difficult thing of all, yet he overcame his reluctance because he feared God.

The Root of Love

According to Eleazar ben Judah, the root of love is to love the Lord. In The Secret of Secrets, *he describes the nature of such love:*

The soul is filled with love, bound with the bonds of love in great joy. This joy chases away all bodily pleasure and worldly delight from his heart. The powerful joy of love seizes his heart so that he continually thinks, 'How can I do God's will?' The pleasures of his children and the company of his wife are as nothing in comparison with the love of God. Imagine a young man who has not been with a woman for a long time. He longs for her; his heart burns for her. Imagine his great love and desire when he cohabits with her; he has so much pleasure when his sperm shoots like an arrow. All this is nothing compared with his desire for God's will, to bring merit to others, to sanctify himself, to sacrifice his life in his love ... The love of heaven in his heart is like the flame attached to the coal. He does not gaze at women; he does not engage in frivolous talk, but he concerns himself only to do God's will, and he sings songs in order to become filled with joy in the love of God.

The Root of Humility

Eleazar ben Judah also describes the root of humility as being that a man keep himself far from the honour paid to nobles. Thus The Secret of Secrets *relates:*

If he sits at the feet of his teacher and knows of a certain problem and appreciates that his teacher or his companion knows of it too, let him allow them to ask and he should remain silent. If they do not ask, he should say, 'So-and-so asks this, and he gave this reply', and he should pay honour to his companion and not take any credit for himself ... A further mark of humility is that a man should always give precedence to his neighbour's name before his own, as the School of Hillel did for the School of Shammai; he should always state his neighbour's reasoning before his own. To sum it all up, he should decrease as far as he possibly can his own honour but increase honour of those who fear the Lord.

The Root of the Precepts

Eleazar ben Judah further describes the root of the precepts as consisting of eight things corresponding to the eight threads of the tzitzit *(prayer shawl). Thus* The Secret of Secrets *states:*

The first thread represents the eyes – they should not see any sin. A man should not be haughty; he should not go after his eyes; he should not wink with them. These are the negative precepts having to do with the eyes. The positive precepts are: 'Only take heed to yourself, and keep your soul diligently, lest you forget the things which your eyes saw' [Deuteronomy 4.9]; 'He will save him that is lowly of eyes' [Job 22.29]; 'And for a memorial between thine eyes' [Exodus 13.9].

The second thread represents the ears: 'Thou shalt not hear a false report' [Exodus 23.1] – not listen to vain words. This is the negative precept. The positive precept is: 'And now, O Israel, harken to the statutes' [Deuteronomy 4.1].

The third thread represents the throat: 'Thou shalt not eat any abominable thing' [Deuteronomy 14.3]. This is the negative precept. The positive precept is to eat unleavened bread on Passover and so forth.

The fourth thread represents the organs of speech – the mouth and the tongue – that these should not utter vain words, for if a man does this he violates a negative precept, as it is written: 'All things toil to weariness; man cannot utter it' [Ecclesiastes 1.8]; 'Thou shalt not take the name of the Lord thy God in vain' [Exodus 20.7]; 'And you shall not swear by my name falsely' [Leviticus 19.12]; 'Nor lie to one another' [Leviticus 19.12]; 'You shall not bear false witness' [Leviticus 19.11]. These are the negative precepts. The positive precepts are: 'And you shall teach them diligently unto your children' [Deuteronomy 6.7]; 'And my tongue shall speak of your righteousness' [Psalms 35.28].

The fifth thread represents the hands: 'Put not your hand with the wicked' [Exodus 23.1]; 'You shall not rob' [Leviticus 19.13]. These are the negative precepts. The positive precepts are: 'You shall surely open your hand' [Deuteronomy 15.8]; 'And you shall bind them for a sign upon your hand' [Deuteronomy 6.8].

The sixth thread represents the feet: 'You shall not go up and down as a talebearer' [Leviticus 19.16]; 'And go not after other gods' [Jeremiah 25.6]; 'And he that hastens with his feet sins' [Proverbs 19.2]. These are the negative precepts. The positive precepts are: 'After the Lord your God you shall walk' [Deuteronomy 13.5]; 'You shall walk in all the ways which the Lord your God has commanded you' [Deuteronomy 5.30]; 'Guard your foot when you go to the house of God' [Ecclesiastes 4.17].

The seventh thread corresponds to the sexual organ: 'You shall not commit adultery' [Exodus 20:13]. This is the negative precept. The positive precepts are: 'And you, be fruitful and multiply' [Genesis 9:7], and circumcision.

The eighth thread corresponds to the nose – anger and stubbornness and smelling the perfumes of idols – as it is written: 'And th shall cleave nought of the devoted thing to thy hand' [Deutero

13:18]. These are the negative precepts. The positive precept is to smell myrtle branches on the Sabbath and so forth.

Let a man remember these eight things. Let them always be in his heart. One – the eyes; two – the ears; three – the tongue; four – the throat; five – the hands; six – the feet; seven – the sexual organ; eight – the nose. He should not sin with any of these and his heart should concentrate on each to plan how to keep these things.

INTENTION IN PRAYER

In their mystical reflections the Hasidei Ashkenaz *were preoccupied by prayer: the Jewish liturgy was compared to the sacrificial offerings of the biblical Temple. The perfection of this service required intense concentration. Yet these pietists accepted that the prayers of simple people – even if they were not in Hebrew or in the required form – were acceptable as long as they were motivated by the right intention. As the classic text of the* Hasidei Ashkenaz, *the* Sefer Hasidim, *explains:*

Every *mitzvah* [commandment] a person can perform should be performed; whatever a person cannot perform, he should think of performing it. This is illustrated by the story of a person who was a shepherd and did not know how to pray. Every day he used to say, 'Sovereign of the universe, you know that if you had cattle to entrust to my care, others I would charge for this; but for you I would do it for nothing because I love you.' . . . Once a learned man passed and he found that this shepherd prayed thus. He said to him, 'You fool; don't pray in this way.' The shepherd asked him, 'How should I pray?' Immediately the learned man taught him the order of prayer, the *Shema* [prayer of divine unity] and the *Amidah* [eighteen benedictions] so that he would not continue to say what he had become used to saying. After this learned man left, he forgot all that he had learned, and he did not pray. What he had been accustomed to say, he became afraid to say because that *zaddik* kept him from it.

One night that learned man was told in a dream, 'If you do not tell him to continue saying what he had been accustomed to say before you met him, and if you do not return, evil will befall you ˑʸ·ou robbed me of one destined for the world-to-come.' At ˑˑˑ·him and asked, 'What is the text of your prayer?' ˑecause I have forgotten what you taught me and ˑt to say [what I used to say] . . . The learned man ˑream: say what you had been used to say.' So we see that it is not Torah and good deeds, but his intention of doing good which is accounted to a person as something great. For God seeks the heart. Therefore shall a person think noble thoughts towards the Holy One, praised be he.

THE *MITZVOT*

The Sefer Hasidim *was also concerned with the importance of ensuring that God's commands* (mitzvot) *were followed.*

It is written in the Torah, 'You shall surely rebuke your neighbour and not bear sin because of him' [Leviticus 19.17]. We are thus obligated to rebuke a fellow Jew who out of desire or laziness fails to keep any of the 248 positive commandments or who violates any of the negative commands. Our sages taught that whoever has the occasion to chastise another Jew for violating a positive or negative precept, and does not do so, is culpable for those offences . . . How do we know that one must persist and criticize him a second time if one is not heeded the first time? This is taught by the following: Whence can we infer that if one has rebuked once, he is to do so again? We may infer it from the verse, 'You shall surely rebuke your neighbour' [Leviticus 19.17]. The person who rebukes must adapt his words to the nature of the one being rebuked – if he is a gentle individual he must be rebuked gently; if he is strong, he must be rebuked according to the gravity of his offences . . . Partiality must not be shown to an elderly or distinguished person, if the one who is rebuking is not to be censured for failing to rebuke the other. Nor is he to show partiality to a teacher . . . The person who is to rebuke others is under an obligation to rebuke himself for his own offences and to mend his ways before criticizing others – otherwise they will not listen to him . . . One must not desist from rebuking his neighbour till he turns him to the right course and he desists from offences in worldly matters and in his relationship to God.

GOOD DEEDS

According to the Sefer Hasidim, *a life of piety embraces moral living in all its dimensions.*

It is forbidden to accustom oneself to flattery. One must beware of saying what he does not mean; instead he must speak what is in his heart – one must match his speech with what he believes. One must not deceive anyone, including a non-Jew ... Similarly one must not pressure another to eat when he knows he will not do so, nor should one give presents to another when he knows he will not accept them. One may not open a barrel of wine suggesting that he is doing so in the other person's honour when the barrel had to be opened in any case ... The same applies to all similar situations – even a single word of deception is forbidden. One must be truthful in speech, upright in spirit, and his heart should be free of all perversity and vanity. One should be a person of integrity in all aspects: one should not be quarrelsome, scornful or mocking ... One is not to indulge in excessive joking, nor be overly sad and grieving. Instead a person must greet everyone in a gracious manner. One should not be ambitious or greedy for wealth, nor lazy and shrinking from work. Rather he should be of a generous eye, modestly pursuing his occupation, engaging in the study of Torah, and taking pleasure in the little that is his portion. One must not be contentious, envious, lusting. Neither should he be desirous of honour, since envy, lust and desire for honour undermine a person's life in the world.

The Hymn of Glory

According to the Hasidei Ashkenaz, *prayer is like Jacob's ladder extending from earth to heaven; it is a process of mystical ascent. It was in this milieu that the Hymn of Glory was composed – a prayer that subsequently gained a central place in the Ashkenazi liturgy. Here the unknowability of God is suffused with a longing for intimacy with the Divine:*

> Sweet melodies will I sing to you
> And hymns compose,
> For my soul yearns for your presence
> To know the mystery of your being.
> When I but bring your praises to my lips
> My love for you wells up within my heart;
> Therefore will I extol you
> And honour your name with songs of adoration.
> I will tell of your glory
> Though I have not seen you;
> I will speak of you in similes
> Though I cannot know your essence.
> You revealed a semblance of your splendour
> In the mystic visions of your faithful servants, the prophets.

They envisioned your grandeur and your might
From the stupendous work of your creation.
They speak of you not as you are
By inference drawn from your handiwork.
They portrayed you in countless forms
That are all but imperfect aspects of your oneness.
They envisioned you as a sage and as a youth.
As a sage sitting in judgement
And as a youth in the day of battle,
As a warrior staking his strength in combat,
Wearing the helmet of victory on his head,
Defeating his foes by his right arm, by his holy might.
I will proclaim his renown,
For he has conferred his love on me,
And he will be to me a crown of splendour.
I see his head luminous as pure gold,
His holy name inscribed upon his forehead.
Adorned by his people with a crown
Of grace and glory, magnificence and beauty.
O may the temple of righteousness,
His noble ornament,
Be remembered in his favour,
May he keep his beloved people in glory,
Crowned with the sovereign diadem of beauty.
His splendour is my renown, and mine is his,
And he is near to me when I call on him.
He revealed the ways of his providence,
To his humble servant Moses
Who glimpsed the fullness of his eternal mystery.
He loves his people,
His humble seed he glorifies,
He who is surrounded by man's praise
Takes delight in them.
The essence of your word is truth;
O you who have called into being the generations
Extend your care to a people that yearns for you.
Receive the multitude of my hymns,
And may the song of my prayer come before you.
Let my prayer be like incense,
Let a poor man's song be to you
As the song once chanted at the altar of sacrifice.
May my prayer come before you,

The sustainer of the universe and its Creator,
The just, the mighty one.
Accept the silent promptings of my heart,
For all my being is astir with longing for your presence.

MYSTICAL STUDY

Parallel with the development of mystical doctrines among the Hasidei
Ashkenaz *in the Rhineland, Jewish mystics in southern France engaged
in speculation about the nature of God, the soul, the existence of evil
and the religious life. In twelfth-century Provence the earliest kabbalistic text, the* Bahir, *reinterpreted the concept of the* sefirot *as depicted
in the* Sefer Yetsirah. *According to the* Bahir, *the* sefirot, *which in the*
Sefer Yetsirah *correspond to the ten basic numbers, are represented as
divine attributes, lights and powers, which fulfil particular roles in the
work of creation. For those scholars study of such doctrines was of paramount importance.*

Whoever turns his heart away from the affairs of the world and
concerns himself with the work of the *merkavah*, it is regarded by
the Holy One, praised be he, as though he had prayed all day . . . Said
Rabbi Rehumei, 'What is the meaning of the verse "The way of life
is the reproof of instruction" [Proverbs 6.23]? This teaches us that
one who studies the work of creation and the work of the Chariot
cannot but stumble, as it is written, "And this stumbling is under
your hand" [Isaiah 3.6]. These are matters that one cannot grasp
unless one stumbles over them, and the Torah calls it, "the reproof
of instruction", but in truth one thereby attains the path of life.'

THE COSMIC TREE

According to the Bahir *the ten* sefirot *are structured as a cosmic tree
from which souls blossom forth.*

All agree that they [the angels] were not created on the first day, so
that they might not say, 'Michael stretched out [the world] in the
south side of the sky, Gabriel in the northern side, and the Holy One,
praised be he, in the middle.' But, 'I the Lord made everything; I
stretched out the heavens myself; I spread out the earth – it was from
me' [Isaiah 44.24]. As written, the Hebrew word for 'from me' means
literally 'Who was with me?'
    'I am the one who planted this tree for the whole world to play
with, and I spread out everything in it, and I called it "all", because

everything is attached to it and everything emerges from it, and all are in need of it. They look to it and wait for it. From it all souls blossom joyously. I was alone when I made it, and no angel can exalt himself over it to say, "I preceded you", for even when I stretched out my land in which I planted and rooted this tree and I caused them to rejoice together, and I rejoiced with them, who were with me and to whom I disclosed this secret.' . . .

'What is this tree that you speak of?'

He said to him, 'It refers to the potencies of God [the *sefirot*] in graded order, and they are like a tree.' As a tree by being watered bears fruit, so the Holy One by means of water increases the powers of the tree.'

'And what is the water of the Holy One, praised be he?'

'It is wisdom. And this refers to the souls of the righteous that are carried from the spring to the great channel and ascend and are attached to the tree.'

'And through what are they carried?'

'Through the people of Israel; when they are righteous and good, the *Shekhinah* [divine presence] abides among them and in their words in the lap of the Holy One, praised be he, and he prospers them and increases them.'

THE BLUE THREAD

The Bahir *also discusses the mystical significance of the blue thread in the* tzitzit *(fringes).*

What is meant by earth? It is the source from which the heavens were formed, and it is the sea of wisdom. Corresponding to it is the thread of blue which is included in the fringe in the corner of a garment [Deuteronomy 22.12]. Rabbi Meir stated, 'Why was blue singled out from all colours? Because blue resembles the sea and the sea resembles the sky, and the sky resembles the throne of divine glory, as it is written, "And they saw the God of Israel and under his feet was as sapphire pavement and as the heavens for purity" [Exodus 24.10], and it is also written, "As the appearance of the sapphire stone so was the appearance of the throne" [Ezekiel 1.26].

'Why do we add a thread of blue in the *tzitzit* and why do we have thirty-two threads? This is comparable to the case of a king who had a beautiful garden in which there were thirty-two paths, saying [to the watchman], "Guard them and walk in them daily and whenever you tread on them, it will be well with you." What did this watchman do? He appointed guardians over them, saying, "If I should remain alone in these paths – it is impossible for one watchman to guard all of them. Moreover, people will say, this king is a miser." Therefore did this watchman appoint other watchmen for each of the paths . . . and why was the thread of blue added? Said the watchman, "Perhaps these watchmen might say, 'This garden is ours'." He gave them a sign and said, "See, this is a sign of the king that the garden is his, and that he established these paths, and they are not mine. Here is his seal."

'To what may this be compared? To a king and his daughter who possessed slaves who wanted to go on a journey, but they feared the king's anger. The king then gave the slaves his seal, but they were afraid of the daughter and she gave them a token. They said, "Now with these two seals [the white and the blue] the promise in the verse will apply 'The Lord will keep you from all evil; he will guard your soul' [Psalms 121.7]."'

TRANSMIGRATION OF SOULS

In the Bahir *the doctrine of the transmigration of souls played an important role in explaining the existence of human suffering:*

Why is it that there is a righteous person who enjoys good, and there is a righteous person who suffers? It is because in the latter case the righteous person was formerly wicked – for this reason he is punished. But is one punished for offences committed during one's youth? Did not Rabbi Simon say that the heavenly tribunal inflicts punishment only for evil conduct that takes place after a person is twenty?

He replied, 'I do not refer to misdeeds in the course of a person's life. I refer to the fact that a person pre-existed prior to his present life.' His colleagues said to him, 'How long will your explanation remain a mystery?' He said, 'Consider the analogy of the person who planted a vine in his garden and hoped they would grow good grapes, but instead they were bad. He realized that he had failed. He therefore planted again, and fenced the new vines after he had removed the bad vines. He planted a second time but realized he had not succeeded. He fenced it in, and planted again after he cleared the bad vines. Yet he saw that he had failed again, removed the bad vines, and tried again.' 'How long does this go on?' He said, 'For a thousand generations as it is written, "The matter which he ordained for a thousand generations" [Psalms 105.8].'

MYSTICISM OF LIGHT

In the Gate of Kavvanah, *Azriel of Gerona depicted the meditative methods used by the Provence school. Here kabbalistic meditation is based on light in which one elevates the mind from one light to a higher one.*

Imagine that you yourself are light, and that all of your surroundings, on every side, are also light. In the middle of this light is a throne of light. Above this throne is a light called *nogah* [glow]. Facing this is another throne. Above the second throne is a light called *tov* [good]. You are standing between the two. If you wish to take revenge, turn to the *nogah*; if you wish to seek mercy, turn to the *tov*. The words that you speak should be directed towards this light. Now turn yourself to the right of it, and there you will find another light. This is a light that is called *bahir* [brilliant]. To its left you will find a light. This is a light called *zohar* [radiant]. Above these two, directly between them, is a light called *kavod* [glory]. Around it is a light called *chaim* [life]. Above it is the crown. This is the light that crowns the desires of the mind and illuminates the paths of the imagination, enhancing the radiance of the vision. This light has no end, and it cannot be fathomed. From the glory of its perfection issues desire, blessing, peace, life and all good to those who keep the way of its unification.

The true path is straight, depending on an individual's concentration. He must know how to concentrate on its truth with attachment of thought and desire derived from its unfathomable power. According to the strength of his concentration, he will then transmit power through his desire, desire through his knowledge, imagination through his thoughts, strength through his effort, and fortitude through his contemplation. When there is no other thought or desire intermingled with his concentration it can become so strong that it can transmit an influence from the *Ayn Sof* (Infinite) . . . An individual thus ascends with the strength of his concentration from one thing to the next, until he reaches the *Ayn Sof.*

KABBALISTIC STUDY

Among the most important figures of the early kabbalah *of the thirteenth century was Abraham ben Samuel Abulafia. After becoming disillusioned with more conventional subjects, he engaged in kabbalistic*

pt to unravel the mystery surrounding God and the
ha-Ot (The Book of the Sign) he explained that
els of kabbalistic study.

at eludes most rabbis who concentrate on talmudic
y divided into two parts. The first deals with knowing
God through the method of the ten *sefirot* called 'plants', so that
whoever effects disunity among the *sefirot* is guilty of cutting down
the plants – it is the *sefirot* that manifest the secret of divine unity.
The other part involves knowing God through the method of the
twenty-two letters of the alphabet . . . These two methods are not
perceived through the senses, nor known as axioms, nor are they
part of commonly accepted knowledge. Thus most scholars are
unaware of them.

Undoubtedly the first category of kabbalistic study must precede
the second, but the second is of greater importance. The latter was
the goal in the creation of the human species. Those who attain it
are the ones whose mental faculties have reached complete self-
realization. It is to them that the Lord of all existence has revealed
himself and disclosed his secret. The first group are called prophets,
and those who know God through his work share this designation
to some extent. Those who are called prophets in this sense meditate
in their hearts on the changing substance of their thoughts, and
their deliberations are purely subjective. The light of God illumines
some of their thoughts, sometimes with a tiny light. They themselves
recognize that this emanates from outside themselves, but they
receive no verbalized message that they should recognize as speech
– it is only light.

But both these groups are prophets who begin by being illumined
with the light of life; from this stage they rise from light to light,
through mediation on the ramification of their thoughts, which are
rendered sweet by their fusion with the divine realm. Through the
enhancement of their merit they approach the highest distinction to
a point where the speech they hear within themselves is linked with
the fountain from which all speech derives. They ascend from speech
to speech until their inner speech is potent in itself and becomes
ready to receive the divine speech, whether it be the form of the
speech, or the contents of the speech itself. These are the true prophets, in justice and in righteousness. Thus the mastery of the knowledge of the ten *sefirot* precedes the additional knowledge of the name
of God and not vice versa.

PROPHECY

Advancing a theory of prophetic mysticism in Sefer
ben Samuel Abulafia believed that through the techn
the letters of various divine names, one could receiv
the Holy Spirit and thereby become a prophet.

Prophecy is a mode of the intellect. It is the expression of the love of the Lord our God, the Lord is one . . . Here is the strong foundation which I deliver to you that you should know it and engrave it upon your heart: the Holy Name, the whole of the Torah, the sacred Scriptures and all the prophetic books; these are all full of divine names and tremendous things. Join one to the other. Depict them to yourself. Test them, try them, combine them . . . First begin by combining the letters of the name *YHVH*. Gaze at all its combinations. Elevate it. Turn it over like a wheel that goes round and round, backwards and forwards like a scroll. Do not set it aside except when you observe that it is becoming too much for you because of the confused movements in your imagination. Leave it for a while and you will be able to return to it later. You can then make your request of it and when you attain to wisdom do not forsake it.

For the initial letters and the final letters, the numerical values, the *notarikons* [numerical calculation of Hebrew letters], the combinations of letters and the permutations, their accents and the forms they assume, the knowledge of their names and the grasping of their ideas, the changing of many words into one and one into many – all these belong to the authentic tradition of the prophets . . . We know by a prophetic divine tradition of the Torah that when the sage who is an adept combines [the letters of the divine name] one with the other, the holy spirit flows into him . . . When you look at these holy letters in truth and reliance and when you combine them – placing that which is at the beginning at the end and that which is at the end at the beginning, and that which is in the middle at the end and so forth in like manner – these letters will all roll backwards and forwards with many melodies.

Let him begin gently and then make haste. Let him train himself to be thoroughly familiar with the changes as they are combined, and it is essential, too, for him to be thoroughly familiar with the secrets of the Torah and the wisdom thereof in order to know that which he brings about through these combinations. Let him

...ken his heart to reflect on the spiritual, divine, prophetic picture.

NUMERICAL COMBINATION

Influenced by the Hasidei Ashkenaz *and the* Súfi *traditions of Islam, Abraham ben Samuel Abulafia wrote meditative texts concerning the technique of combining the letters of the alphabet as a means of realizing human aspirations towards prophecy. In his* Sefer Hayyei ha-Olam ha-Ba (The Book of the Life of the World to Come), *he explained the technique of such numerical combination.*

Make ready to direct the heart to God alone. Cleanse the body and choose a lonely house where no one shall hear your voice. Sit there in your closet and do not reveal your secret to any person. If you can, do it by day in the house, but it is best if you complete it during the night. In the hour when you prepare to speak with the Creator and wish him to reveal his might to you, then be careful to abstract all thought from the vanities of the world. Cover yourself with your prayer shawl and put *tefillin* [phylacteries] on your head and hands that you may be filled with awe of the *Shekhinah* that is near you. Cleanse your clothes and if possible let all your garments be white, for all this is helpful in leading the heart towards the fear and love of God. If it is night, kindle many lights, until they are bright. Then take ink, pen and a table and remember that you are about to serve God in joy of the gladness of heart.

Now begin to combine a few of many letters, to permute and to combine them until you heart is warm. Then be mindful of their movements and of that you can bring forth by moving them. And when you feel that your heart is already warm and when you see that by combinations of letters you can grasp new things, which by human tradition or by yourself you would not be able to know, and when you are thus prepared to receive the influx of divine power which flows into you, then turn all true thoughts to imagine his exalted angels in your heart as if they were human beings sitting or standing about you . . . Having imagined this very vividly, turn your whole mind to understand the many things that will come into your heart through the letters imagined. Ponder them as a whole and in all their detail, like one to whom a parable or a dream is being related, or who meditates on a deep problem in a scientific book, and try thus to interpret what you shall hear that it may as far as possible accord with your reason.

THE PRONUNCIATION OF GOD'S NAME

After mastering the technique of letter manipulation
Abraham ben Samuel Abulafia's system involved the pro..
God's name. This method was presented in Or Ha-Sekhal (The ̣
of the Intellect). *The system contained in this work involved the com-*
bination of the four letters of God's name (yod, hey, vav, hey) *with the*
letter aleph *pronounced with the five vowels.*

Make yourself right. Meditate in a special place where your voice
cannot be heard by others. Cleanse your heart and soul of all other
thoughts in the world. Imagine that at this time your soul is separating itself from your body, and that you are leaving the physical world
behind so that you enter the future world that is the source of all
life. [The future world] is the intellect, which is the source of all
wisdom, understanding and knowledge, emanating from the King
of Kings, the blessed Holy One . . . Your mind must then come to
his mind, which gives you power to think. Your mind must divest
itself of all other thoughts other than his thought . . . This is the
technique.

When you begin to pronounce the *aleph* without any vowel, it is
expressing the mystery of unity [*Yichud*]. You must therefore draw
it out in one breath and no more. Do not interrupt this breath in
any manner whatsoever until you have completed the pronunciation
of the *aleph*. Draw out this breath as long as you extend a single
breath. At the same time, chant the *aleph*, or whatever other letter
you are pronouncing while depicting the form of the vowel point.
The first vowel is the *holem* above the letter. When you begin to
pronounce it, direct your face towards the east, not looking up or
down. You should be sitting, wearing clean, pure white robes over
all your clothing, or else wearing your prayer shawl over your head
and crowned with *tefillin*. You must face east since it is from that
direction that light emanates.

With each of the twenty-five letter pairs, you must move your
head properly. When you pronounce *holem*, begin facing directly
east. Purify your thoughts, and as you exhale raise your head little
by little until when you finish your head is facing upwards. After
you finish, prostrate yourself on the ground . . . Just as you faced
upwards when pronouncing the *holem*, face downwards when you
pronounce the *hirek*. In this manner you draw down the supernal
power and bind it to yourself. When you pronounce the *shurek*, do
not move your head upwards or downwards. Instead move it straight
forwards . . . When you pronounce the *tzere*, move your head from

left to right. When you pronounce the *kametz*, move it from right
to left.

LETTER COMBINATION

An anonymous follower of Abraham ben Samuel Abulafia composed
Shaarei Tzedek (The Gates of Justice), *in which he explained that his
master taught him the method of letter combination.*

After two months had passed and my thought had disengaged
itself, I became aware of strange phenomena taking place within me.
I set myself the task at night of combining letters with each other
and of meditating on them . . . I continued for three nights without
telling him. The third night, after midnight, I nodded off, quill in
my hands and paper on my knees. Then I noticed that the candle
was about to go out. I rose to put it right as often happens to a person
who is awake. Then I saw that the light continued. I was greatly
astonished, as after close examination, I saw that it came from
myself. I said, 'I do not believe it.' I walked to and fro all through
the house, and behold the light was with me. I lay on a couch and
covered myself up, and behold, the light was with me all the while.
I said, 'This is truly a great sign and a new phenomenon that I have
perceived.'
   The next morning I communicated it to my teacher, and I brought
him the sheets which I had covered with combinations of letters. He
congratulated me and said, 'My son, if you would devote yourself to
combining holy names, still greater things would happen to you.
And now, my son, admit that you are unable to bear not combining.
Give half to this and half to that. That is, do combinations half the
night, and permutations half the night.' I practised this method for
about a week.
   During the second week the power of meditations became so
strong that I could not manage to write down the combination of
letters . . . and if there had been ten people present they would not
have been able to write down so many combinations as came to me
during the influx. When I came to the night in which this power
was conferred on me, at midnight – when this power especially
expands and gains strength whereas the body weakens – I set out to
take up the great name of God, consisting of seventy-two names,
permuting and combining it.
   But when I had done this for a little while, behold, the letters took
on in my eyes the shape of great mountains; strong trembling seized

me and I could summon no strength, my hair stood on end, and it was if I were not in this world. At once I fell down, for I no longer felt the least strength in any of my limbs. And behold, something resembling speech emerged from my heart and came to my lips and forced them to move . . . When I got up in the morning I told my teacher about it. He said to me, 'And who was it that allowed you to touch the name. Did I not tell you to permute only letters?' He spoke on, 'What happened to you represents indeed a high stage among prophetic degrees.'

THE ORIGIN OF GOD'S NAMES

Pre-eminent among early Spanish kabbalists in the thirteenth and fourteenth centuries was Joseph Gikatilla, who studied under Abraham ben Samuel Abulafia, later developing his own style of kabbalah. In his Ginat Egoz (The Nut Garden), *he discussed the hidden meanings of the names of God. In a later work,* Shaarei Orah (The Gates of Light), *he outlined the significance of the names of God on the basis of categories derived from the ten* sefirot. *The names of God, he argued, stem from the primary name, YHVH.*

Truth and the tradition of the covenant dictate that whoever wishes to gain his ends by means of the names of the Holy One, praised be he, must study with all his strength the teachings of the Torah concerned with each of the holy names mentioned there, like *Ehyeh, Yah, YHVH, Adonai, El, Eloah, Elohim, Shaddai* and *Tzevaot* . . . Know that all his holy names mentioned in the Torah are all dependent on the four-letter name, *YHVH.* You might ask, 'Is not the name *Ehyeh* the basis and the source of all?' Then know that the four-letter name is like the body of the tree, while the name *Ehyeh* is the root of the tree, from which more roots spread and branches reach out on all sides. All other holy names are like branches and leaves that spread from the body of the tree, and each of the branches bears its own fruit.

THE TEN *SEFIROT* AND THE DIVINE NAMES

Joseph Gikatilla's Shaarei Orah *contains an exposition of the ten* sefirot *and the divine names that are associated with them. This scheme is represented diagrammatically as follows:*

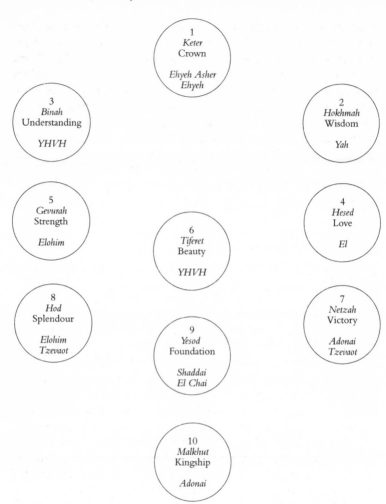

CONTEMPLATION OF THE DIVINE NAMES

According to Joseph Gikatilla in Shaarei Orah, *the words and divine names associated with the* sefirot *serve as guides, enabling one to ascend through meditation on the ladder of the* sefirot.

You have asked me, my brother, beloved of my soul, to enlighten you regarding the path involving God's names so that through them you will gain what you wish and reach what you desire . . . if one wishes

to attain what he desires through the use of God's names, he
first study the Torah with all his might, so that he can grasp
meaning of every one of God's names mentioned in the Torah. Thes
names are *Ehyeh, Yah, YHVH, Adonai, El, Eloah, Elohim, Shaddai,*
and *Tzevaot.* One must know and understand that each of these
names is like a key for all of his needs . . . When a person contemplates these names, he will find that the entire Torah and all the
commandments depend on them. If one knows the meaning of all
these names, he will understand the greatness of him who spoke and
brought the universe into being. He will fear God, yearning
and pining to bind himself to him through his knowledge of
these names.

ASCENDING THE *SEFIROT*

In Shaarei Orah *Joseph Gikatilla provided an explanation of the
method of ascending the* sefirot *(divine emanations).*

The first name is closest to all created things. It is through this name
that one enters the presence of God the King . . . this name is
Adonai . . . This is the lowest level of the Divine . . . There are three
names, one above the other. *Adonai* is on the bottom, *YHVH* is in
the middle, and *Ehyeh* is on top. It is from the name *Ehyeh* that all
kinds of sustenance emanate, coming from the source, which is the
Infinite, *Ayn Sof.* It then proceeds through a series of steps until it
reaches the blessed name, *YHVH.* From the name *YHVH* all spiritual channels flow and the flux is transmitted to the name *Adonai.*
    One who attaches himself to *Adonai* is worthy of eternal
life . . . One who wishes to perceive eternal life should attach himself
to the attribute of *El Chai.* This means that through his prayers, one
should bring *El Chai* into *Adonai* . . . When the attribute *Yesod,*
which is called *El Chai,* is bound to *Adonai* [*Malkhut*], then one can
draw down all his needs . . . We must bind the *sefirot* together,
attaching all levels through the attribute of *Adonai* [*Malkhut*] . . . One
must elevate his concentration higher and higher. He must probe
deeper than the future world until he reaches the level of *Keter*
[crown], which is *Ehyeh,* which is associated with the *Ayn Sof.* One
who wishes to attain from God what he desires must contemplate
the ten *sefirot.* He must transmit will and desire from the highest to
lowest, until he brings it to the final desire, which is the name
Adonai. The *sefirot* are then blessed through him, and he is blessed
through the *sefirot.*

NDIFFERENCE

emporary of Abraham ben Samuel Abulafia and
a master of letter combinations. According to
nce to all external influences is a prerequisite to
...nus he wrote in The Light of the Eyes:

When an individual is worthy of the mystery of attachment to God, he can also be worthy of the mystery of stoicism. After he is worthy of stoicism, he can also be worthy of meditation. And after he is worthy of meditation, he can be worthy of enlightenment. From there he can reach the level of prophecy where he can actually predict the future. In explaining the mystery of stoicism, Rabbi Abner related the following story:

A sage once came to one of the meditators and asked that he be accepted into their society. The other replied, 'My son, blessed are you to God. Your intentions are good. But tell me, have you attained stoicism?' The sage said, 'Master, explain your words.' The meditator said, 'If one man is praising you and another is insulting you, are the two equal in your eyes or not?' He replied, 'No, my master, I have pleasure from those who praise me, and pain from those who degrade me. But I do not take revenge or bear a grudge.' The other said, 'Go in peace my son. You have not attained stoicism. You have not reached a level where your soul does not feel the praise of one who honours you, nor the degradation of one who insults you. You are not prepared for your thoughts to bound on high, that you should come and meditate. Go and increase the humbleness of your heart, and learn to treat everything equally until you have become stoic. Only then will you be able to meditate.'

THE LETTERS OF THE TETRAGRAMMATON

In The Light of the Eyes *Isaac of Acco explained that one should constantly have the letters of the Tetragrammaton (God's name) before one's eyes in pursuing the path of enlightenment.*

You should constantly keep the letters of the unique name in your mind as if they were in front of you, written in a book with the Torah script. Each letter should appear infinitely large. When you depict the letters of the unique name in this fashion your mind's eye should gaze on them, and simultaneously your heart should be directed towards the Infinite Being [*Ayn Sof*]. Your gazing and thought should be as one. This is the mystery of true attachment, concerning which the Torah says, 'To him shall you attach yourself' [Deuteronomy 10.20].

If you are able to do this, no evil will befall you; you will not be subject to errors caused by logic or emotion, and you will not be the victim of accidents. As long as you are attached to God, you are above all accident, and in control of events . . . You might ask why one should bind his thoughts to the Tetragrammaton more than to any other name. The reason is that this name is the cause of causes and the source of all sources. Included in it are all things, from *Keter* to the lowliest gnat. Blessed be the name of the glory of his kingdom for ever and ever.

RESPONSA FROM HEAVEN

In Responsa from Heaven *Jacob of Marvège submitted questions to heaven before he went to sleep after fasting and engaging in letter manipulation. Perplexed about the order of the sections of the* tefillin, *he addressed a query to God requesting that the angels provide a response.*

I asked another question. This is what I asked, 'O great, mighty and awesome King, wise in secrets, revealing mysteries, telling hidden things, keeping the covenant of mercy, let your mercy be great this day and command the holy angels to pass on information regarding the doubts we have concerning the correct order of the sections of the *tefillin*. Some authorities say that the sections beginning with "And it shall come to pass" have to be in the middle, otherwise the *tefillin* are unfit; other authorities say that the sections have to be placed in the order in which they occur in Scripture, otherwise the *tefillin* are unfit for use. Now, O King of Kings, command your holy angels to inform me of the correct ruling preferred by you.'

They replied, 'Both opinions are the words of the living God. Just as there is a debate on earth, so is there a debate on high. The Holy One, blessed be he, holds that these sections have to be in the middle, but all the heavenly family holds that the sections have to follow the order in which they appear in Scripture.'

GOD'S NAME OF FORTY-TWO LETTERS

In another passage of in Response from Heaven *Jacob of Marvège asked if it was permissible to use the holy name of forty-two letters to request the angels to make a person wise in learning.*

I asked another question, 'Is it permitted to make theurgic use of the holy name of forty-two letters to conjure the holy angels appointed over the Torah to make a man wise in all that he studies and never forget his learning? Is it permissible to conjure by means of the name the angels appointed over wealth and victory over enemies and in order to find grace in the eyes of princes? Or is it forbidden to make use of the name for any of these purposes?'

They replied, ' "Holy, holy, holy is the name of the Lord of hosts" [Isaiah 6.3]. He alone will satisfy all your needs.'

Ayn Sof

The greatest mystical work of the Middle Ages was the Zohar. *Although the author placed this rabbinic source in a second-century setting, focusing on Rabbi Simeon bar Yohai and his disciples after the Bar Kokhba uprising, the doctrines of the* Zohar *are of much later origin. Written in Aramaic, the text is largely a* midrash *in which the Torah is given a mystical or ethical interpretation. Drawing on the kabbalistic doctrine, the* Zohar *depicts the* Ayn Sof *as beyond human knowledge.*

Rabbi Eleazar asked Rabbi Simeon, 'We know that the whole-offering is connected to the Holy of Holies so that it may be illumined. To what heights does the attachment of the will of the priests, the Levites and Israel extend?' He said, 'We have already taught that it extends to *Ayn Sof* since all attachment, unification, and completion is to be secreted in that secret which is not perceived or known, and which contains the will of all wills. *Ayn Sof* cannot be known, it does not produce end or beginning like the primal *ayin* [nothing], which does bring forth beginning and end . . . there are no end, no wills, no lights, no luminaries in *Ayn Sof.*'

The Nameless Ayn Sof

The Ayn Sof *is the cause of all, but the* Zohar *states that it has no name because it transcends creation.*

Master of the worlds, you are the cause of causes, the first cause who waters the tree with a spring; this spring is like the soul to the body, since it is like the life of the body. In you there is no image, nor likeness of what is within, nor of what is without.

You created heaven and earth, and you have produced from them sun and moon and stars and plants, and in the earth, trees and grasses and the Garden of Eden and wild beasts and fish and men so that through them the upper realms might be known, as well as how the upper and lower realms are governed and how the upper and lower realms might be distinguished.

There is none that knows anything of you, and besides you there is no singleness or unity in the upper or the lower worlds. You are acknowledged as Lord over all. As for all the *sefirot*, each one has a known name and you are the perfect completion of them all. When you remove yourself from them, all the names are left like a body without a soul.

AYN SOF BEYOND PERCEPTION

The Zohar *declares that the* Ayn Sof *is beyond all comprehension; it encompasses all worlds, but cannot be encompassed.*

He understands all, yet there is none that understands him. He is not called by the name *yod, hey, vav, hey,* nor by any other name except when his light extends itself upon them. When he removes himself from them, he has no name of his own at all. 'That which is exceedingly deep, who can find it?' [Ecclesiastes 7.24]. No light can look upon him without becoming dark. Even the supernal *Keter* – whose light is the strongest of all levels and of all the hosts of heaven, both the upper and the lower realms – is alluded to in, 'He made darkness his hiding place' [Psalms 18.12]. While of *Hokhmah* (wisdom) and *Binah* (understanding) it is said, 'Clouds and thick darkness surround him' [Psalms 97.2]. This is even truer of the remaining *sefirot*, and even truer of the *hayyot*, and even truer of the elements that are dead bodies. He encompasses all worlds and none. But he surrounds them on every side, above and below and in the four corners of the globe; none may go beyond his domain. He fills all worlds, but no other fills him.

EMANATION OF THE AYN SOF

According to the Zohar, *the process of emanation is revealed in Scripture – here the* Ayn Sof *is described as the source of all that exists.*

At the very beginning the King made engravings in the supernal purity. A spark of blackness emerged in the sealed within the sealed, from the mystery of the *Ayn Sof*, a mist within matter, implanted in a ring, no white, no black, no red, no yellow, no colour at all. When he measured with the standard of measure, he made colours to provide light. Within the spark, in the innermost part, emerged a source, from which the colours are painted below; it is sealed among the sealed things of the mystery of *Ayn Sof*. It penetrated, yet did not penetrate its air. It was not known at all until, from the pressure of its penetration, a single point shone, sealed, supernal.

Beyond this point nothing is known, so it is called *reshit* [beginning]: the first word of all. 'And they that are wise shall shine as the brightness [*zohar*] of the firmament and they that turn the many to righteousness as the stars for ever and ever' [Daniel 12.3]. *Zohar*, sealed among the sealed, made contact with its air, which touched, but did not touch, the point. Then the *reshit* extended itself, making a palace for itself, for glory and praise. There it sowed the holy seed in order to beget offspring for the benefit of the world. This mystery is in 'the holy seed shall be its stock' [Isaiah 6.13].

Zohar, which sowed seed in its own honour like the seed of the silkworm that makes fine purple fabric, is the one that covers itself within; it makes a palace for itself that brings praise to it and benefit to all. With this *reshit* the sealed one, which is not known, created this palace. This palace is called *Elohim* [God] – this mystery is in *Bereshit bara Elohim* ['In the beginning God created' (Genesis 1.1)]. *Zohar* is that from which all the words were created through the mystery of the expansion of the point of this concealed brightness.

Action of the *Ayn Sof*

The Zohar *further states that the* Ayn Sof *is the source of all that exists.*

He brings everything from potentiality into actuality; he varies his deeds but there is no variety in him. It is he that puts the *sefirot* in order; there are among the *sefirot* great, intermediate and small. Each has its place in the order, yet there is no order in him. He created everything with *Binah*, but there is none that created him. He is a designer, designing everything with *Tiferet* [beauty], but he has no design or designer. He formed everything with *Malkhut* [kingdom], but there is none that formed him. Since he is within these ten *sefirot*, he created, designed and formed everything with them. There he places his unity, so that they might recognize him there.

Whoever separates one *sefirah* from its fellow among these ten *sefirot* called *yod, hey, vav, hey,* makes, as it were, a separation within him. It is he that unites *yod* with *hey* and *vav* with *hey*, and they are called *yod*, *hey*, *vav*, *hey* only because of him; similarly with the letter of the *Adonai*, and *Ehyeh* and *Elohim*. But as soon as he removes himself from there he has no known name.

It is he that binds all the chariots of the angels, and binds them together; and he supports the upper and the lower worlds. And were he to remove himself from them they would have neither sustenance, knowledge or life. There is no place where he is not, above and without end, and below without limit, and on every side there is no God but he. But despite the fact that he is in every place, he did not place his *Beriyah* (creation), *Yetsirah* (formation) and *Asiyah* (making) in the Throne, nor among the angels, nor in the heavens, nor in the earth, nor in the sea, nor in any created being in the world, so that all creatures might recognize him in the *sefirot*. Although he created, formed and made everything through them, the names *Beriyah*, *Yetsirah* and *Asiyah* do not apply to them, as they do to the lower worlds, but rather are they the way of emanation.

THE PROCESS OF EMANATION

According to its mystical interpretation, the first verse of the creation account contains a description of the engraving of the hidden things and the sustaining of the lower sefirot. In this process the Hebrew letters and vowels of the forty-two-lettered name play a central role. As the Zohar recounts:

Thus far the secret of the innermost mystery which he engraved, built, sustained in a concealed way through the mystery of one verse. From now on *bereshit bara shit* [in the beginning he created six] 'from the one end of heaven to the other' [Deuteronomy 4.32], the six extremes that extend from the supernal mystery through the extension he created from the primal point, *bara*. Here was engraved the mystery of the 42-lettered name. 'And they that are wise shall shine' like the musical accents.

The vowel-points follow them in their singing, moving at their behest, like an army at the behest of the king. The letters are the body; the vowel-points are the spirit. All of them in their travels follow the accents, standing in their place. When the singing of the accents moves, the letters and the vowel-points move after them; when it stops, they do not move but remain in their stations. 'And they that are wise shall shine' – letters and vowel-points; 'as the brightness' – the singing of the accents; 'of the firmament' – the extension of the singing, like those that prolong and continue the singing; 'and they that turn the many to righteousness' – these are the pauses among the accents that stop their travels as a result of which speech is heard; 'shall shine' – that is, the letters and the vowel-points; and they will shine on their travels in a concealed mystery on a journey by hidden paths [Deuteronomy 12:3]. All extends from this.

CREATION THROUGH LIGHT

The first chapter of Genesis depicts the creation of light as the first act. In its mystical interpretation of this passage the Zohar *stresses the role of light in the unfolding of God's purposes.*

This light is a sealed mystery: the expansion that extended itself and burst through from the secret mystery of the hidden supernal air.

First of all, the expansion burst through and produced a single hidden point from its own mystery. Thus did *Ayn Sof* burst out of its air and reveal a single point: *yod*. Once that *yod* had extended itself, whatever remained of the mystery of the hidden air was light. When the first point, *yod*, was discovered by it, it then appeared to it touching but not touching. Once it had extended itself, it emerged as the light, a remnant of the air – 'the light that had already existed' [*Bereshit Rabbah* 3:2].

This light existed; it emerged and removed itself and was hidden, and one single point of it remained. It has continuous contact in a secret way with this point, touching and not touching, illuminating it by means of the primal point which emerged from it. Therefore all hangs together. It illuminates on this side and on that. When it ascends everything ascends and is incorporated with it. It reaches and is concealed in the place of *Ayn Sof* and all is made one.

The point of light is 'Light'. It expanded, and seven letters of the alphabet shone on it but they did not solidify, they were moist. Then darkness emerged and another seven letters of the alphabet emerged but they did not solidify and remained moist. The firmament emerged and dissipated the division between the two sides, and another eight letters emerged from it, making twenty-two in total. The seven letters on this side and the seven letters on that side drew together. They were all engraved in the firmament and stayed moist. The firmament solidified; the letters solidified and they assumed their different shapes, and the Torah was engraved there in order to give some light to the realms outside.

AYN SOF AND THE SEFIROT

According to the Zohar *the* Ayn Sof *is not one in number – in this regard it is unlike the* sefirot, *each of which is part of a unity of ten. It is through the process of emanation that the* sefirot *emerged from the* Ayn Sof *and guide the universe.*

Elijah said, 'Master of the world, you are one but not in number. You are the highest of the high, the secret of all secrets. You are altogether beyond the reach of thought. You are he that produced ten *tikkunim* [restorations], which are called the ten *sefirot*, so that through them you might guide the secret worlds that are not revealed. Through them you are concealed from humanity. You bind them and unite them. Since you are within, whoever separates one of the ten from its fellow is thought of as making a separation in you.'

THE ORDER OF THE SEFIROT

The Zohar *explains that the* sefirot *emanate successively from above to below, each one revealing a stage in the process.*

In this same fashion has the cause of causes derived the ten aspects of his being, which are known as *sefirot* and named the crown and the source, which is a never-to-be-exhausted fountain of light. As a result he designates himself *Ayn Sof*, the Infinite. Neither shape nor form has he, and no vessel exists to contain him, nor any means to comprehend him. This is referred to in the words, 'Refrain from searching the things that are too hard for you, and desist from seeking for that which is hidden from you.'

Then he shaped a vessel small as the letter *yod*. He filled it from him and called it 'wisdom-gushing fountain', and called himself wise because of it. And afterwards, he fashioned a large vessel named sea and designated it 'understanding' and himself understanding on its account. He is both wise and understanding in his own essence, whereas wisdom in itself cannot claim such a title – only through him who is wise and has made it full from his fountain; thus understanding in itself cannot claim that title – only through him who filled it from his essence; it would be turned into an aridity if he were to depart from it. In this respect it is written, 'As the waters fall from the sea, and the river is drained dry' [Job 14.11].

Finally, 'He smites the sea into seven streams' [Isaiah 11.15]. That is, he directs it into seven precious vessels which he calls Greatness, Strength, Glory, Victory, Majesty, Foundation, Sovereignty. In each he designates himself thus: great in Greatness, strong in Strength, glorious in Glory, victorious in Victory, 'the beauty of our maker' in Majesty, righteous in Foundation [Proverbs 10.25]. All things, all vessels, and all worlds does he uphold in Foundation. In the last, in Sovereignty, he calls himself King, and his is 'the greatness, and the strength, and the glory, and the victory, and the majesty; for all that is in heaven and in earth is yours; yours is the kingdom, O Lord, and you are exalted as head above all' [1 Chronicles 29.11].

In his power lie all things, be it that he chooses to reduce the number of vessels, or to increase the light issuing therefrom, or the contrary. But over him there exists no deity with power to increase or reduce. Further, he made beings to serve these vessels: each a throne supported by four columns with six steps to the throne. In all ten. Altogether, the throne is like the cup of benediction about which ten statements are made in the Talmud, harmonious with the Torah, which was given in ten words, and with the ten words by which the world was created.

THE COSMIC STRUCTURE OF THE *SEFIROT*

The Zohar *explains that the* sefirot *are arranged in the form of a human body.*

You are the one who guides the *sefirot*, and there is no one to guide you neither above, nor below, nor on any side. You have prepared garments for them from which the souls fly to the children of men. Several bodies are prepared for them, which are called 'body' in respect of the garments that cover them. They are named in this arrangement: *Hesed* [Love] – right arm; *Gevurah* [strength] – left arm; *Tiferet* [beauty] – torso; *Netzah* [victory] and *Hod* [splendour] – two legs; *Yesod* [foundation] –the completion of the body, the sign of the holy covenant; *Malkhut* [kingdom] – mouth, which we call the oral Torah. The brain is *Hokhmah* [wisdom], the inner thought; *Binah* [understanding] is the heart . . . The supernal *Keter* [crown] is the crown of royalty . . . it is the headpiece of the *tefillin*.

THE *SITRA AHRA*

In the Zohar, *the* sitra ahra *(other side) is viewed as opposed to divine abundance and grace. It should be conceived of as a counter-*sefirot, *a realm of dark, unclean powers opposed to holiness and goodness.*

At the beginning of the night, when darkness falls, all the evil spirits and powers scatter abroad and roam about the world and the *sitra ahra* sets forth and enquires the way to the King from all the holy sides. As soon as the *sitra ahra* is roused to this activity here below, all human beings experience a foretaste of death in the midst of their sleep. As soon as the impure power separates itself from the realm above and descends to begin its rule here below, three groups of angels are created who praise the Holy One in three night watches – one following another, as the companions have pointed out. But while these sing hymns of praise to the Holy One, the *sitra ahra* . . . roam about here below, even into the uttermost parts of the earth. Until the *sitra ahra* has thus departed from the upper sphere, the angels of light cannot unite themselves with their Lord.

The Shell of Evil

According to the Zohar, *evil is like the bark of a tree of emanation; it is a husk or shell in which the lower dimensions of existing things are encased. As the* Zohar *relates:*

King Solomon, when he penetrated into the depths of the nut garden, took a nut shell [*kelippah*] and drew an analogy from its layers to these spirits that inspire sensual desires in human beings, as it is written, 'and the delights of the sons of men are male and female demons' [Ecclesiasticus 2.8]. This verse also indicates that the pleasures in which men indulge in the time of sleep give birth to multitudes of demons. The Holy One, blessed be he, found it necessary to create all these things in the world so as to ensure its permanence, in order that there should be, as it were, a brain with many membranes encircling it. The whole world is constructed on this principle – upper and lower, from the first mystic point up to the furthest removed of all the stages. They are all coverings one to another, brain within brain, and spirit within spirit, so that one is a shell to another.

The Upper and Lower Spheres

In explaining the picture of divine creation, the Zohar *adopted a Neoplatonic conception of a ladder of spiritual reality composed of four worlds in descending order:* Atzilut *(emanation),* Beriyah *(creation),* Yetsirah *(formation), and* Asiyah *(making). The pattern of the* sefirot *is reflected in each of the lower worlds. In the realm of Asiyah, where the individual's soul attempts to achieve perfection, the sefirot are symbolized by various forces, including the rainbow, the dawn, trees, grass and the sea, and all of these natural phenomena are linked to the upper spheres.*

It is written, 'You rule the proud swelling of the sea; when the waves thereof arise, you still them' [Psalms 89.10]. When the stormy waves of the sea mount on high, and beneath them yawn the chasms of the deep, the Holy One, blessed be he, sends down a thread from the 'right side', which in some mysterious way restrains the mounting waves and calms the rage of the sea. How is it that when Jonah was cast into the sea, and had been swallowed by a fish, his soul did not at once leave his body? The reason is that the Holy One, blessed be he, has dominion over the swelling of the sea, which is a certain thread from the 'left' that causes the sea to heave and rises with it. If it were not for the thread of the 'right side', it would never be removed, since as soon as this thread descends into the sea and is fairly grasped by it, then the waves of the sea are stirred up and begin to roar for prey until the Holy One, blessed be he, thrusts them back to their own place.

THE IMAGE OF HUMANKIND

For the kabbalists, the doctrine of a hidden God who brings about creation had important implications for the kabbalistic view of humankind. The biblical idea that human beings were created in the image of God implies that they were modelled on the sefirot: they are a microcosm reflecting the nature of the cosmos. As far as souls are concerned, they consist of three faculties. The lowest is the nefesh *(soul, the gross side of the soul), and from the* nefesh *springs all movements, instincts and physical desires. The next faculty is the* ruah *(spirit), which constitutes the moral element. Finally,* neshamah *(super-soul) is the rational component. As the* Zohar *explains:*

The *nefesh* stands in intimate relation to the body, nourishing and upholding it; it is below, the first stirring. Having acquired due worth, it becomes the throne for the *ruah* to rest upon, as it is written, 'until the spirit be poured upon us from on high' [Isaiah 32.15]. When these two – soul and spirit – have duly readied themselves, they are worthy to receive the *neshamah*, resting in turn upon the throne of the spirit. The *neshamah* stands pre-eminent and is not to be perceived. There is throne upon throne, and for the highest a throne.

The study of these grades of the soul yields an understanding of the higher wisdom; it is in such fashion that wisdom alone affords the linking together of a number of mysteries. It is *nefesh*, the lowest stirring, to which the body adheres just as in a candle flame the obscure light at the bottom adheres close to the wick without which it cannot exist. When fully kindled, it becomes a throne for the white light above it. When these two come into their full glow the white light becomes a throne for a light not wholly discernible, an unknowable essence reposing on the white light and so in all there comes to be a perfect light.

It is the same with the man that arrives at perfection and is named 'holy', as the verse says, 'for the holy that are in the earth' [Psalms 16.3]. It is likewise in the upper world. Thus when Abram entered the land, God appeared before him, and Abram received *nefesh* and there erected an altar to the like grade. Then he 'journeyed toward the south' [Genesis 12.9] and received *ruah*. He attained at last to the summit of cleaving to God through *neshamah*, and thereupon he 'built an altar to the Lord' [Genesis 12:7], whereby is meant the ineffable grade which is that of *neshamah*. Then seeing that he must put himself to the test, and pass through the grades, he journeyed into Egypt. There he resisted being seduced by the demonic essences, and when he had proved himself, he returned to his abode, and actually he 'went up out of Egypt' [Genesis 13.1]. His faith was strong and reassured, and he attained to the highest grade of faith. From that time, Abram knew the higher wisdom, and he cleaved to God – of the world he became the right hand.

TIKKUN

The soul has a central role in the cosmic drama of repairing the disharmony in the world that was due to Adam's sin. Through the cutting off of the sefirah *kingdom from the other* sefirot, *the* sitra ahra *attained dominance. Yet human beings can bring about* tikkun *(restoration) since their souls can ascend towards the angels. As the* Zohar *explains, human action has a profound effect on the higher worlds.*

It is from below that the movement starts, and thereafter is all perfected. If the community of Israel failed to initiate the impulse, the One above would also not move to go to her. It is thus the yearning from below which brings about the completion above.

KAVVANAH

The kavvanah (intention) involved in mystical prayer is seen as a necessary element, in the mystery of heavenly unification that brings the sefirot to the lowest realm and ties them to each other and to the Ayn Sof. Thus the Zohar states:

So prayer is made up of both action and speech; when the action is faulty, speech does not find a spot to rest in. Such prayer is not prayer, and the man offering it is defective in the upper world and the lower. The main thing is to perform the act and give utterance to words in co-ordination with it; this is the perfect prayer . . . Both upper and lower worlds are blessed through the man who performs his prayer in a union of action and word and thus effects a unification . . . This service must be performed by the man with full devotion of heart. Then the Holy One, blessed be he, will take pity on him and forgive his sins. Happy is the man who knows how to persuade, as it were, and how to offer worship to his master with devotion of will and heart.

DEVEKUT

The supreme rank attainable to the soul at the end of its sojourn is the mystical cleaving to God (devekut). In this quest prayer is of fundamental importance. Thus the Zohar states:

Happy is the portion of whoever can penetrate into the mysteries of his master and become absorbed into him, as it were. Especially does a man achieve this when he offers up his prayer to his master in intense devotion, his will then becoming as the flame, inseparable from the coal, and his mind concentrated on the unity of the higher firmaments, and finally on the absorption of them all into the most high firmament. Whilst a man's mouth and lips are moving, his heart and will must soar to the height of heights, so as to acknowledge the unity of the whole, in virtue of the mystery of mysteries in which all ideas, all wills, and all thoughts, find their goal, that is, the mystery of the *Ayn Sof.*

3 Post-Medieval Mysticism
c.1300–c.1750

Introduction

In the post-medieval world Jewish scholars continued to explore mystical doctrines found in early sources. Such kabbalists included the fourteenth-century mystic Abraham ben Isaac of Granada who was preoccupied with the mystical significance of the Hebrew letters. One of the most important kabbalists of the sixteenth century was Joseph Tzayach who formulated meditative doctrines of a unique character. Another major figure of this period was the halakhic scholar Joseph Caro, who joined a kabbalistic circle in Safed. According to tradition, he received communications from a *maggid* (divine messenger), which he identified as the soul of the *Mishnah* (law) as well as the *Shekhinah* (Divine Presence).

Another sixteenth-century Safed mystic, Moses Cordovero, interpreted the teachings of early mystics and propounded his own kabbalistic theories. Cordovero's work constitutes a systematic summary of the *kabbalah* up to his own time, and in his most important treatise, *Pardes Rimonim* (*Orchard of Pomegranates*), he outlined the Zoharic concepts of the Godhead, the *sefirot* (divine emanations), the celestial powers and the earthly processes.

Later in the sixteenth century, kabbalistic speculation was transformed by the greatest mystic of Safed, Isaac Luria. Of primary importance in the Lurianic system is the mystery of creation. For Luria, creation was a negative event: the *Ayn Sof* (Infinite) had to bring into being an empty space in which creation could occur, since divine light was everywhere, leaving no room for creation to take place. This was accomplished by the process of *tzimtzum* (divine contraction) – the contraction of the Godhead into itself. Thus the first act of creation was not positive, but rather one that demanded withdrawal.

After this first act, a line of light flowed from the Godhead into empty space and took the shape of the *sefirot* in the form of *Adam Kadmon* (primal man). In this process divine lights created the vessels (the extended shapes of the *sefirot*), yet they were not strong enough to contain pure light and so shattered. The teachings of Luria were subsequently transmitted by his most important disciple, Hayyim Vital. In the next century another major kabbalistic figure, Moses Hayyim Luzzatto, declared he was the recipient of divine communications from a *maggid*, which he passed on to a circle of mystics who engaged in messianic speculation.

The Vowel Points

Following the compilation of the Zohar, *Jewish scholars continued to elaborate mystical doctrines. Pre-eminent among such mystical reflection was the treatise,* Berit Menuhah (The Covenant of Rest), *attributed to Abraham ben Isaac of Granada – in all likelihood this work was composed in Spain during the fourteenth century. Like Abraham Abulafia, the author of this treatise was preoccupied with the letters of the Tetragrammaton. In his view this name of God should have the vowel segol (composed of three dots). Such pointing, he believed, represents the unification of all things with their divine source.*

As for the seventh manner of pointing, who can speak of its profundity, power, wisdom and mighty wonders of its processes and stages, great . . . and terrible, showing forth wisdom and knowledge. This more than all the other illuminations . . . points to the unity of the Holy One, blessed be he. As this illumination ascends on high, it combines the fire on high with the fire below and in turn it combines the fire on high with the power of its source and thereby combines all things. As it descends, it combines those on high with those below, joining form to form.

For the truth is that man's form is that of the Supernal Form, Supernal Man. So too vermin and creeping things and all things have their supernal forms . . . in its great brilliance, this illumination pushes away at first the other illuminations but then brings them near again by its great power, attracting them by its abundant splendour. This demonstrates how great it is, having neither beginning nor end.

When this illumination issues forth to spread from the well-known beautiful and choice root, without any admixture, exceedingly clear and terrible, it ascends by way of the path leading to Beth-El. It gains power in its ascent and is divided into three parts. These three parts join each creature with its source and thereby domination is ascribed to the master of each. As for these three parts – the first attaches each to its place, all the beings on high; the second attaches each to its place, all the middle beings; the third joins together all the beings below, one by one, to the power of their source, so that all dominions become a single dominion. This dominion is bound to the one Lord so that the tent is joined to become one.

Two of these three illuminations ascend at the same pace but the third moves forward powerfully between the other, equally paced, two. The third which should be higher in fact turns face downwards, taking hold of its two companions to draw them down, with the great power it possesses even when it faces downwards.

Three Illuminations

Abraham ben Isaac of Granada maintained in Berit Menuhah *that the three illuminations represented by the three dots were actually one, yet they became divided into three. In* Berit Menuhah *he explained that the middle one was the most powerful and provided the unifying principle.*

These three illuminations are called the places of those illuminations that form the peculiar treasure with which Israel has been endowed . . . By the power of their holiness the two illuminations that proceed apace together, with the third attached to them, go forth until they reach the place of Massah and Taberah.

There they increase in strength until a further illumination proceeds from him who brings all things into existence; this scatters the illuminations in all directions. At the end of a day and a watch, the third illumination, covered by Massah and still holding fast to the other two, seizes hold of them in order to gather them together again, restoring them so that they regain their previous excellence. Here if only you can understand it, you will discover a profound mystery. For this illumination is situated among the scattered ones of Israel; as these are gathered together you will observe exceedingly profound wisdom, very plausible matters. The accents are *segol* and then *zarka segol*. You must prepare yourself to grasp a matter of exceedingly great wisdom and you will discover such a perfect unification that neither your fathers nor your fathers' fathers ever comprehended.

The Three Points and Redemption

The three points of the vowel segol *were separate, yet they formed a unity, representing the redemptive power. Thus Abraham ben Isaac of Granada wrote in* Berit Menuhah.

These three illuminations – bound all three one to the other – appear as three types of dominion, one joining energetically together the upper beings, the second the middle beings, and the third the lower beings. Since these three dominions are found together, they appear as a single entity bound to the First Cause. All the functions of these three illuminations are carried out energetically. As a result, the vowel is a short one, moving energetically towards the First Cause.

These are the three illuminations that rise on behalf of Israel to gather them together from the lands of their Dispersion among their enemies. These are exceedingly significant illuminations.

Another great illumination proceeds from these. From this latter, those forces of destruction and harm that caused Judah and Israel to be scattered from their land draw their nourishment. These three illuminations are not nowadays in operation and will not be until a day and a watch has passed, namely, the sign of the Redemption, shoutings of grace. Grace unto it. For when that day comes, Redemption will spread abroad to all the corners of the earth, from the rising of the sun to the going down thereof.

The Segol and Messianic Impulses

In Abraham ben Isaac of Granada's system in Berit Menuhah *the vowel* segol, *when applied to the Tetragrammaton, activates messianic impulses.*

Happy the person who continues in his uprightness to walk in the good path, keeping far from the wicked in those days. Perhaps he will be saved from the troubles known as the birth-pangs of the Messiah. Of the time of redemption it is said, 'And I will spur Egypt against Egypt; and they shall fight every one against his brother, and every one against his neighbour, city against city, and kingdom against kingdom' [Isaiah 19.2]. Afterwards there will be such peace and tranquillity, such rest and quiet, that no generation prior to that of the Messiah could have imagined it, neither the generation of the wilderness nor that of King Solomon . . . Who can speak of the wisdom, power and dominion of these three illuminations, which will gather in the dispersed of Israel at the time of Redemption?

THE HIGH PRIEST

In the Berit Menuhah *Abraham of Granada explained that the mystical method of using vowels was employed by the High Priest when he entered the Holy of Holies on the Day of Atonement; when he pronounced the divine name pointed with the vowel* segol *he was granted a vision of the* Shekhinah *and the sefirotic tree (the tree of divine emanations).*

Know that the name the High Priest uttered on the Day of Atonement was pointed entirely with short vowels as you now see. He uttered the name very slowly. When he set the first consonant in motion, he did so with force bringing it to and fro, to east, north, south and west with incomprehensibly powerful movements. When he uttered the second consonant, he drew all the illuminations together with an exceedingly great force. When he uttered the third consonant, he did so hurriedly in order to prevent the quality of power from becoming so strong that it would destroy the world. When he uttered the fourth consonant, he did so hurriedly in order to prevent the quality of rest becoming so strong that there would be insufficient power for the world to continue to exist in its present form.

I shall explain to you the pointing used by the High Priest when he uttered the name on the Day of Atonement . . . the High Priest would pronounce the name as it is written *YHVH* together with its vowels, and gently and mysteriously he would meditate on it . . . How glorious was the High Priest when he emerged safely from the Holy Place, for the radiance of the *Shekhinah* was as a halo around his head and remained with him until he reached his home.

KABBALISTIC CHIROMANCY

One of the most important kabbalists of the sixteenth century was Joseph Tzayach. Born in Jerusalem, he served as a rabbi in Damascus and frequently travelled to Jerusalem, where he wrote The Onyx Stone *in 1538. This work was designed as a meditative text containing complex numerical calculations, associating the ten* sefirot *with the fingers. Here the upper nine* sefirot *are arranged according to the conventional kab-balistic pattern – but the lowest* sefirah *is represented by the heart line of chiromancy:*

The line on the palm that begins under the middle finger and extends to the little finger indicates the coronet (*Malkhut*). This goes 'to the east of Ashur' [Genesis 2.14], encompassing the ten holy *sefirot*. Surrounding them are the ten unclean ones. All of this is alluded to in the lines of the palm, and is understood by those who know these mysteries.

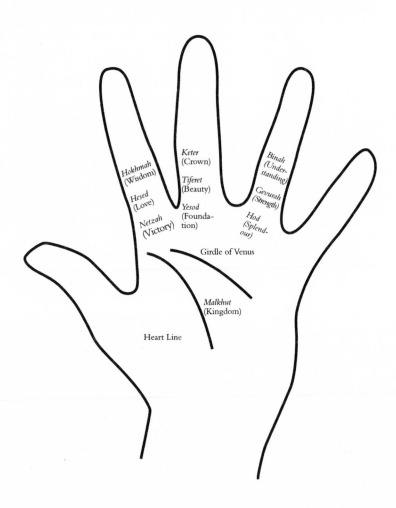

THE MAGIC SQUARES

In Tzayach's system in The Onyx Stone, *numerical magic squares are associated with the* sefirot *– they are used for a very special meditation where each horizontal row is a house, and each number represents a 'room'. Thus in the magic square of the tenth order which represents* Keter, *the first room of the first 'house' is 1, the second room is 2, the third is 98, and the fourth 97. In his meditative scheme, each number represents a 'thousand myriad'* parsangs (a form of measurement), *and a 'thousand myriad' coloured lights. As one travels from room to room and from house to house proceeding through this magic square, one must attempt to depict these lights.*

MAGIC SQUARE OF ORDER TEN CORRESPONDING TO *KETER*

1	2	98	97	96	5	94	93	9	10
90	12	13	87	86	85	84	18	19	11
80	79	23	24	76	75	27	28	22	71
70	69	68	34	36	35	37	33	62	61
41	59	58	57	45	46	44	53	52	50
51	49	48	47	55	56	54	43	42	60
31	32	38	64	65	66	67	63	39	40
30	29	73	74	25	26	77	78	72	21
20	82	83	14	16	15	17	88	89	81
91	92	3	7	6	95	4	8	99	100

THE PROPHETIC POSITION

In meditating on the magic squares, Tzayach argued in The Onyx Stone *that one must use the prophetic position where one places one's head between the knees. In this way it is possible to ascend to the heavenly heights.*

If you wish to enter into this mystery, concentrate on all that we have said. Contemplate the rooms that we have discussed, together with their lights, colours and letter combinations. Meditate on this for a while, either briefly or at length. Begin by placing your head between your knees.

PRAYING IN THE PROPHETIC POSITION

In The Onyx Stone, *Tzayach included the prayer that should be recited when in the prophetic position:*

> *Ehyeh Asher Ehyeh* [I shall be what I shall be],
> crown me [*Keter*].
> *Yah* [God], grant me wisdom [*Hokhmah*].
> *Elohim Chaim* [Living God], grant me understanding [*Binah*].
> *El* [God], with the right hand of his love,
> make me great [*Hesed*].
> *Elohim* [God], from the terror of his judgement,
> protect me [*Gevurah*].
> *YHVH* [Lord], with his mercy, grant me beauty [*Tiferet*].
> *Adonai Tzevaot* [Lord of Hosts], watch me forever [*Netzah*].
> *Elohim Tzevaot* [God of Hosts], grant me beatitude from
> his splendour [*Hod*].
> *El Chai* [Living God], make his covenant my foundation
> [*Yesod*].
> *Adonai* [Lord], open my lips and my mouth will speak
> your praise [*Malkhut*].

THE DIVINE *MAGGID*

Another major figure of the post-medieval period was Joseph Caro, who emigrated to Turkey after the expulsion of the Jews from Spain. Believing himself to be the recipient of a heavenly mentor (maggid), *he identified this* maggid *with the soul of the* Mishnah *and the* Shekhinah. *According to Solomon Alkabetz, in* Maggid Mesharim *the revelations of a* maggid *took the form of utterances through Caro to the circle of mystics.*

No sooner had we studied two tractates of the *Mishnah* than our Creator smote us so that we heard a voice speaking out of the mouth of the saint, may his light shine. It was a loud voice with letters clearly pronounced. All the companions heard the voice but were incapable of understanding what was said. It was an exceedingly pleasant voice that became increasingly strong. We all fell on our faces and none of us had any spirit left in him because of our great fear and awe. The voice began addressing us, 'Friends, choicest of the choice, peace to you, beloved companions. Happy are you and happy those who bore you. Happy are you in this world and happy in the next that you resolve to adorn me on this night. For these many years had my head fallen with none to comfort me. I was cast down to the ground to embrace the dunghills but now you have restored the crown to its former place . . . Behold I am the *Mishnah*, the mother who chastises her children and I have come to converse with you.'

THE MEMBERS OF THE HEAVENLY ASSEMBLY AND ELIJAH

In his Maggid Mesharim (Teller of Upright Words), *Caro described the revelations that he received from the* maggid *concerning the heavenly assembly and the prophet Elijah.*

Then slumber came upon me, and I slept for about half an hour. I awoke in distress since he did not converse with me at length as previously. I began once more to rehearse the *Mishnah* and before I completed two chapters, the voice of my beloved began to knock in my mouth, saying, 'Although you imagined I had forsaken you and left you, do not think I really will leave you before I have fulfilled my promise not to withhold good from your mouth. You must cleave to me and to the fear of me, as I have said, and then you will be elevated, lifted up, and made high before all the members of the heavenly academy, all of whom send you greetings because you busy yourself all the time with the Talmud and the codes and combine the two.

'As I have said, you should also mortify your flesh so as to have the merit of seeing Elijah face to face while you are yet awake. He will speak to you mouth to mouth and will greet you, since he will become your teacher in order to teach you all the mysteries of the Torah. Open your eyes, therefore, and dedicate all your thoughts to my worship and the fear of me.'

FORETELLING THE FUTURE

In the Maggid Mesharim *Joseph Caro described the revelations he received from the* maggid *about the course of his future life. Thus he wrote:*

If you behave as I instruct you, I will give you the merit of completing your books, commentaries and works in which you decide the law, without error or mistake. I shall allow you to print them and publish them in all the borders of Israel as you have requested of the Lord your God . . . And I shall give you from this modest and worthy wife a saintly and wise son, for she deserves it because of all she suffered. As for you, if you do as I have taught you to separate yourself from all worldly pleasure, and if you will sanctify yourself in purity during the marital act, behaving as it was said of Rabbi Eliezer, that he engaged in the act as if a demon were compelling him to do it, then you will be worthy of bringing down into the world a pure, holy soul from the Garden of Eden and he will become a great sage and saint.

When she will have departed this life you will marry, one after the other, two women who had been previously married . . . From these you will have sons gifted with discernment, knowing his name and studying his Torah for his own sake. I shall increase the fame of your college in both quality and quantity.

And after all this I shall give you the merit of being burned for the sanctification of my name . . . All the saints in the Garden of Eden, the *Shekhinah* at their head, will come out to meet you, welcoming you with many songs and praises . . . The Holy One, blessed be he, and his academy have sent me to tell you these mysteries in order that you might see yourself occupying such a stage.

Sefirot and Colours

Moses Cordovero, a student of Joseph Caro, was one of the most important kabbalists of sixteenth-century Safed. A member of an ascetic circle of mystics, Cordovero composed several important mystical treatises including Pardes Rimonim (The Orchard of Pomegranates) *and* Or Neerav (Pleasant Light). *In his* Pardes Rimonim, *he advocated a system of meditation whereby one can bind oneself to the* sefirot. *Such a technique, he believed, is enhanced when colours are used.*

In many places in kabbalistic texts and in the *Zohar*, we find various colours parallel the *sefirot*. One should be extremely careful and not imagine this is to be taken literally. Colour is something physical used to describe the physical world, and the *sefirot* which are not spiritual, should not be depicted with physical properties. If a person believes these are literally the colours of the *sefirot*, he destroys the entire system and oversteps the boundaries fixed by the ancients. One who looks into this should be very careful not to assume that anything physical is implied; rather these colours allude to the results that are transmitted from the highest roots. For example, *Gevurah* [strength] is responsible for victory in war. Because this involves bloodshed [where blood is spilt], it is suitable to ascribe the colour red to this *sefirah*. The colour red likewise expresses hatred, anger and fury.

We therefore ascribe red to the place of judgement. Moreover, everything that is red is derived from the power of this root . . . Likewise the colour white indicates mercy and peace. This is because people with white hair are usually merciful . . . There is no question that things that are white emanate from the power of this root . . . This then is the proper interpretation of the relationship between the colours and the *sefirot*. The colours are used allegorically to allude to their functions and results . . . There is no question that the colours can thus serve as a door to the dynamics of the *sefirot*.

THE UNIFICATION OF THE *SEFIROT*

According to Moses Cordovero, an individual should seek to unify the sefirot. *Thus* Pardes Rimonim *states:*

If one is pure and upright in deed, and if he grasps the cords of love existing in the holy roots of his soul, he will be able to ascend to every level in all the supernal universes . . . When a person is upright and righteous, he can meditate with suitable thoughts and thereby ascend through the levels of the transcendental. He must unify the levels of his soul, joining one part to another, drawing the different levels of his soul to vest themselves in one another. It thereby becomes like a single candelabrum made up of different parts joined together.

The individual must then unify the *sefirot*, bringing them to bind themselves together with a strong knot. He and his soul thus become a channel through which the *sefirot* can exert influence. All of them, from the highest to the lowest, act together through the powerful cord that unites them. When a person binds his soul to the supernal soul through his *Mishnah*, this causes the roots to be bound together with a strong knot.

MEDITATION ON THE *SEFIROT*

In Pardes Rimonim *Cordovero explained how it was possible to meditate on the* sefirot. *Here he stressed that such meditation should focus on the Tetragrammaton (God's name).*

When a person thinks about any one of the attributes, it is inevitable that he will separate it from the others. In his mind he imagines a separate attribute, distinct from all the rest. This is certainly not proper because they must be unified . . . It is necessary to recognize that the *Ayn Sof*, the blessed King of Kings, cannot be encompassed by any name or word. It is incorrect to speak of any attributes in this essence, since it does not change and cannot be described. It cannot be altered, first having one desire and then another, or first engaging in one activity and then another.

Therefore, when one meditates on the *Ayn Sof*, he should not call it *El*, or *Eloah*, or *Elohim*, or give it any other name. All of these names pertain only to the *sefirot* . . . One should not direct his intention towards the *sefirot*, heaven forbid, since one who does so falls into a deep pit . . . The words are therefore appellations for the various attributes in the *sefirot*; they are adjectives pertaining to God. The intent, however, is directed only towards the *Ayn Sof* who is clothed in the *sefirot* and makes use of them . . . This does not mean that one should meditate on the *sefirot* or try to imagine them, since this is impossible . . . Rather, it means that the *sefirot* are associated with ten names spelt with the four letters of the Tetragrammaton. These names are only differentiated by their vowels . . . One who meditates should concentrate on these names. He should keep in mind that nothing can allude to the attribute he seeks other than the Tetragrammaton that is depicted in his mind. These consist of the four letters vocalized in the appropriate manner.

MYSTICAL STUDY

In his Or Neerav *Cordovero defended kabbalistic study against those who were critical of it.*

We have noted that those who keep away from this knowledge can be divided into three groups. Some shun it, saying that there is no need to believe in a secret dimension of the Torah . . . At times they look upon everything according to its literal meaning, having no interest in hidden things, for who can force them to believe in the ten *sefirot* and other branches of this knowledge? They only want to believe in the wondrous unity. If they should be exposed to some aspects of this knowledge, particularly if they hear references to the *Ayn Sof* and different levels of meaning of the Torah, they become unreservedly abusive . . .

There is a second category of individuals who spurn knowledge, and their position is compounded by various arguments. They all agree in their esteem for this knowledge, yet some argue that it is so exalted that not all are worthy to be involved with it. They even feel justified to strike out against those who pursue it. They claim that they are avenging the honour of the Lord of Hosts and the honour of his Torah against those who venture to step into an exalted realm and speculate about divine matters – a topic remote from mortal minds . . .

There is a third group that keeps away from this knowledge by arguing that a person is prone to err in these subjects and commit a sin by falling into one of those errors concerning the divine . . . The group whose approach is acceptable consists of those who follow the right course. They have attained some mastery in the Bible, and in the *Gemara* [Talmud] with its teachings, which have the same status for us as the *Mishnah*; and they have attained some mastery in this knowledge.

They study it for its own sake so as to enter its secrets, to know their Creator, and to attain the wonderful quality of reaching the true understanding of the teaching of the Torah, of praying before the Creator, to effect unification between God and his *Shekhinah* through the performance of his commandments.

LURIANIC *KABBALAH*

In the sixteenth century kabbalistic speculation was transformed by the greatest mystic of Safed, Isaac Luria. Originally brought up in Egypt where he studied the Talmud and engaged in business, Luria withdrew to an island on the Nile where he meditated on the Zohar *for seven years. In 1569 he arrived in Safed, and died two years later after having passed on his teachings to a small group of disciples. According to his disciple Hayyim Vital, Luria was able to penetrate the deepest secrets. Thus Vital wrote in* Etz Hayyim (The Tree of Life).

The Ari [Isaac Luria] was overflowing with Torah. He was thoroughly expert in the Bible, *Mishnah*, Talmud, *pilpul* [talmudic interpretation], *midrash* [rabbinic commentary], *aggadah* [biblical commentary], the workings of creation and the workings of the *merkavah* [the divine chariot]. He was adept in the conversation of trees, the conversation of birds and the speech of angels. He could also read faces in the manner outlined in the *Zohar*. He could discern everything that any individual had done, and could see what they would do in the future. He was able to read people's thoughts frequently before they even entered the individual's mind. He knew future events, and was conscious of everything happening here on earth as well as what was decreed in heaven.

In addition, he knew the mysteries of reincarnation: who had been born previously and who was here for the first time. He could look at a person and explain how he was connected to the Supernal Man and how he was related to Adam. He could read wondrous things in the light of a candle or the flame of a fire. With his eyes he gazed and could see the souls of the righteous, those who had died recently or those who had lived in ancient times. With these he studied the true mysteries that were lying in his bosom, ready to be used whenever he desired. He did not have to meditate to seek them out . . . None of this came through the practical *kabbalah* . . . Instead it came automatically as a result of his piety and asceticism after many years of study, in both the ancient and newer kabbalistic texts. He then increased his piety, asceticism, purity and holiness until he reached a level whereby Elijah would constantly reveal himself to him, speaking to him 'mouth to mouth' and teaching him these mysteries.

DIVINE CONTRACTION

Of primary importance in the Lurianic system is the mystery of creation. In Luria's view, the Ayn Sof *had to bring into being an empty space in which creation could occur. This was accomplished by the process of* tzimtzum – *the contraction of the Godhead into itself as recorded in Hayyim Vital's Etz Hayyim.*

In Luria's view, after the act of withdrawal a line of light flowed from the Godhead into the tehiru *(empty space) and took the shape of the* sefirot *in the form of* Adam Kadmon. *In the process of emanation divine lights created the vessels – the external shapes of the sefirot – which gave specific characteristics to each divine emanation. Yet the vessels were not strong enough to contain such pure light and they shattered. According to Luria, this breaking of the vessels brought disaster and upheaval to the emerging emanations. In explaining the purpose of* tzimtzum, *Luria pointed out that the* Ayn Sof *before creation was not completely unified – there were elements in it that were potentially different from the rest of the Godhead. The* tzimtzum *separated these different elements from one another. After this contraction occurred a residue was left behind. As Hayyim Vital explained in his* Etz Hayyim.

Know that before the emanations emerged and the creatures were created, the simple supernal light of the *Ayn Sof* filled all these, and there was no empty area at all, namely, an empty atmosphere and a vacuum. All was filled with that infinite light. It had neither beginning nor end. All was simple light in total sameness . . . When in his

simple will it was resolved to create worlds and send out the emanations, to bring to objective existence the perfection of his deeds, and
his names and his appellations, which was the reason for the creation
of the worlds, then he contracted himself in the middle point in
himself, in the very centre. He contracted that light; it was withdrawn to the sides around the middle point. Then there was left an
empty space, an atmosphere, and a vacuum extending from the
precise point of the centre.

The contraction was equally distributed around that middle
empty point in order that the vacuum was circular on all sides
equally. It was not in the shape of a square with fixed angles because
the *Ayn Sof* also contracted himself in a circular fashion in equal
proportions on all sides. The reason for this was because the light of
the *Ayn Sof* is equally pervasive. It was thus necessary that it contract
itself in equal measure on all sides . . . There was another reason for
this. It was for the sake of the emanations that were due to be sent
out thereafter in that vacuum . . . By being in the form of circles, the
emanations could all be equally close and attached to the *Ayn Sof*.
They could all receive in equal measure the light and the influences
they needed from the *Ayn Sof* . . . The purpose of this contraction
was to bring to light the source of judgement to act in the worlds.
After this contraction . . . when a vacuum was left, an empty atmosphere through the meditation of the light of the *Ayn Sof*, blessed be
he, there was now available an area in which there could be the
emanations, the beings created, formed and made.

REINCARNATION AND *IBBUR*

*In Isaac Luria's system reincarnation plays a central role in the process
of perfection. As his disciple Jacob Zemah recorded in the* Shulkhan
Arukh Shel Ari (The Set Table of Isaac Luria):

'Thus you shall do with every lost object of your brother'
[Deuteronomy 22.3]. Know that an individual may at times be perfected through *ibbur* [impregnation] and at times he may require
gilgul [reincarnation], which is more painful. The penalty for anyone
who finds a lost object, but does not return it, is that he will not find
justification through *ibbur* after his death. Rather he must return it
in a form of *gilgul*. This is the meaning of the concluding section of
the above verse: 'You may not hide yourself.' This refers to *ibbur* by
itself, which involves being concealed in his neighbour's soul. He will
require *gilgul*, which is more painful than *ibbur*.

THE PUNISHMENT OF *GILGUL*

According to Isaac Luria, if a person does not observe the mitzvot *(commandments) or engage in exegetical study, he will be subject to* gilgul *(reincarnation). Thus his disciple Jacob Zemah wrote concerning his teaching in* Shulkhan Arukh Shel Ari*:*

If a person has not perfected himself by fulfilling all the 613 commandments in action, speech and thought, he will be subject to *gilgul* . . . Also whoever had not studied the Torah according to the four levels indicated by *p r d s*, which is a composite of the words *peshat* [literal], *remez* [allegorical], *derash* [homiletical] and *sod* [mystical], will have his soul returned for reincarnation in order that he might fulfil each of them.

PARTZUFIM

After being shattered, the vessels were rectified and rebuilt. Partzufim *(configurations), each consisting of 613 parts, parallel the 193 parts of the body as well as the 613 commandments. Subsequently they were able to interact with each other anthropomorphically, as well as with human beings, through the Torah. As Hayyim Vital explained in* Etz Hayyim, *in their rectified state as* partzufim *the vessels were able to receive God's light.*

Partzufim

Partzuf	*Sefirah* (Divine Emanations)
Atika Kadisha (The Holy Ancient One)	Upper *Keter* (Crown)
Atika Kadisha (Ancient of Days)	Upper *Keter* (Crown)
Arikh Anpin (Long Face)	Lower *Keter* (Crown)
Abba (Father)	*Hokhmah* (Wisdom)
Ima (Mother)	*Binah* (Understanding)
Zer Anpin (Small Face)	The Next Six
Nukva (Female)	*Malkhut* (Kingdom)

FOUR TETRAGRAMMATONS

In Luria's system as presented by Hayyim Vital in Etz Hayyim, *there was a fifth universe above* Atzilut *(emanation),* Beriyah *(creation),*

Yetsirah *(formation) and* Asiyah *(making), corresponding to the apex of the* yod *in the Tetragrammaton. For Luria this was the realm of another* partzuf, *Adam Kadmon. Within this fifth universe, there are four levels paralleling the four letters of the Tetragrammaton. These four levels manifest themselves in the four letters of the Tetragrammaton, the four lower* partzufim *of* Atzilut *and in the four universes themselves. They are also represented by the accent marks, vowel points, letter decorations, and the letters.*

Four Tetragrammatons

Value	Name	Level
72 *(Ab)*	*YOD HEY VYU HY*	*Hokhmah* (Wisdom)
63 *(Sag)*	*YOD HY VAV HY*	*Binah* (Understanding)
45 *(Mah)*	*YOD HA VAV HA*	The Six
52 *(Ben)*	*YOD HH VV HH*	*Malkhut* (Kingdom)

Levels of Expression

Universe	Expression
Asiyah	Letters
Yetsirah	Ornaments
Beriyah	Vowel Points
Atzilut	Cantellation Notes

MEDITATION ON IMMERSION

In addition to his formulation of theoretical kabbalah, *Isaac Luria proposed a series of meditations related to particular religious practices. Such meditative activity brings a person into the upper universes and involves combinations of divine names and numerology. For example, concerning immersion, he stated in* Shear HaKavanot:

This is a meditation for immersing before the Sabbath. After entering a lake, river or *mikveh* [ritual bath], but before immersion, meditate on the word *mikveh*. Meditate that the *mikveh* is the mystery of the name *Ehyeh* [I shall be] expanded through the letter *hey*.

aleph hey yod hey

This expression has a numerical value of 151 – this is also the numerical value of the word *mikveh* . . . Now meditate on the word *nachal*, meaning stream. This supernal stream consists of seven names. These are the four expansions of the Tetragrammaton: *Ab, Sag, Mah* and *Ben,* together with the three expansions of *Ehyeh,* respectively with the *yod,* the *hey* and the *aleph.* Bring the *mikveh* into this stream. Meditate on these seven names when they are not expanded:

YHVH

YHVH

YHVH

YHYH

AHYH

AHYH

AHYH

Each of these contains a single *yod.* Therefore in the seven names, there are a total of seven *yods.* These seven names are the mystery of the seven names of the Sabbath . . . You must meditate on the simple spelling of the seven names which contain seven simple *yods* – at the same time you must also meditate on the expanded forms. To the seven names, add the name *YaH.* This name is the mystery of the Sabbath. You have a total of eight *yods.* These eight *yods* add up to eighty. This is the numerical value of the letter *nun* and *lamed* from the word *nachal,* the stream . . . Now meditate on the *yods* in groups. There are two such groups. You must therefore meditate on the number two. The word *nahal* has a numerical value of eighty-eight. Add this to the two and you have ninety. This is the numerical value of *mayyim,* meaning water. In this manner you have brought water into the *mikveh.*

Yichudim

For Isaac Luria the aim of meditation is to attain yichudim *(unifications) where one manipulates the letters of God's name. In some cases the names are intertwined and various vowel points are added. Since the divine names reflect spiritual forces which have counterparts in the human psyche, the* yichudim *can have a powerful psychological impact. As Hayyim Vital described in* The Gate of the Holy Spirit:

The lower soul is from the universe of *Asiyah* [making], which is associated with the name *Adonai* [Lord]. One should therefore meditate on the name *Adonai*, binding it to the name *YHVH* [God] in the universe of *Asiyah*. He should then bind this to the name *Ehyeh* [I shall be] in the universe of *Asiyah*. He should then meditate on this, elevating the name *Ehyeh* of *Asiyah*, and binding it to *Adonai* of *Yetsirah* [formation] it should then be bound to *YHVH* [Lord] of *Yetsirah*. One proceeds in this manner through the universes of *Yetsirah*, *Beriyah* [creation] and *Atzilut* [emanation] step by step until he reaches *Ehyeh* of *Atzilut*. He should then bind *Ehyeh* of *Atzilut* to the very highest level, which is the Infinite Being of *Ayn Sof*.

ELEVATION OF THE SOUL

For Isaac Luria it is possible to elevate one's soul at night. As Hayyim Vital explained in The Gate of the Holy Spirit, *it is not necessary to follow all the methods – only one is sufficient. If one does this, then one's soul will ascend on high for that night alone. There are several methods:*

The first method is that on that particular day, the individual should have perfect *kavvanah* [intention] in his prayers . . . such an individual can certainly have his soul rise at night, ascending to 'God's mountain, his holy place'. The second method involves giving charity properly on that day – this means that he should not know to whom he is giving, and the recipient should not have any knowledge from whom he is receiving . . . The third method involves wearing *tefillin* the entire day . . . The fourth method involves 'bringing merit to the guilty'. On that day, one should prevent a wicked person from committing some sin and bring him to repent that one sin . . . The fifth method involves concentrating and recalling every sin that one had done the entire day.

ENLIGHTENMENT

As Hayyim Vital explained in The Gate of the Holy Spirit, *Isaac Luria taught that enlightenment is attainable by following certain practices.*

My master, of blessed memory, told me that a person's prime intention when studying Torah should be to bring enlightenment and the highest holiness to himself . . . One must thus concentrate on binding one's soul to its highest root through the Torah and attaching it there. His intent should be that in this way the rectification of the

Supernal Man should be accomplished. This was God's ultimate plan when he created man and commanded him to study the Torah. There are other qualities that one should cultivate. These include humbleness, humility and the fear of sin ... There are also traits that should be avoided ... these include pride, anger, temper, frivolity and malicious gossip. Even if one has a good reason to exhibit his temper, he should avoid it. One should also avoid idle chatter, although it is not as serious as the five things mentioned above. One should not display temper, even to the members of one's family. Keep the Sabbath in action and speech, with all its particulars. This is very helpful for enlightenment. Sit in the synagogue with awe and trembling. The special meditation for this is of great use in attaining *Ruah Hakodesh* [Holy Spirit].

My master also taught that the prime path of *Ruah Hakodesh* is through care and *kavvanah* in the blessing over food. In this fashion one dispels the power of the *kelippot* [powers of evil] that have a hold on food and attach themselves to the person who eats it ... It is also important to wake up at midnight and recite the Eleventh Psalm ... It is also important to have a set order of study each day and not miss it. This should include the Bible, *Mishnah*, Talmud and *kabbalah*, together with the proper meditations ... My master also said that it is good for a person to live in a house with windows open to the heavens so that he can always lift his eyes to the heavens and gaze at them ... My master also told me that the root of all when it comes to enlightenment is the study of law.

YECHUDIM AND THE SAINTS

In Isaac Luria's view, when the saints meditated through a yichud *(unification), the universes united as Hayyim Vital wrote in* The Gate of the Holy Spirit; *this could happen both at death and during a saint's lifetime.*

There are many saints who meditated with *yichudim* during their lifetime; they knew how to time this so that it would be accepted by the Supernal Will. At such times they would make use of *yichudim* and transmit great benefit to themselves ... Usually when a saint dies, he causes all the universes to unite. But there are saints who knew how to use *yichudim* at auspicious times, and they could do this even during their lives. What other saints could accomplish only after death, they could do while they were still alive.

MEDITATION ON A *YICHUD*

In his teaching, as recorded by Hayyim Vital in The Gate of the Holy Spirit, *Isaac Luria provided a description of the method of meditation.*

It is very beneficial to meditate on a *yichud* while lying prostrate on the grave of a saint. When you do so, contemplate that through your own position, you are causing the saint to prostrate his soul and infuse the bones in his grave. This causes him to come to life in a sense, since his bones become like a body for the soul that infuses them . . .

If you are not on a grave, but meditate on *yichudim* at home, you need not have this intent. But at all times, whether on a grave or at home, it is helpful to contemplate that your soul and that of the saint are bound together, with your soul included in his, and that the two of them are ascending together.

EXPANSION OF THE TETRAGRAMMATON

In his discussion of the yichudim, *Isaac Luria declared that there are four ways to expand the Tetragrammaton. Thus Hayyim Vital wrote in* The Gate of the Holy Spirit:

It can be expanded with *yods* like this to form *Ab*, having a numerical value of seventy-two:

YOD HY VYV HY . . .

It can be expanded to form *Sag* which has a numerical value of sixty-three:

YOD HY VAV HY

It can be expanded with *alephs* to form *Mah* having a numerical value of forty-five:

YOD HA VAV HA

It can be expanded with *heys* to form *Ben* having a numerical value of fifty-two:

YOD HH VV HH

The Tetragrammaton expanded with *yods*, adding up to seventy-two, motivates the union of *Hokhmah* [wisdom – father] and *Binah* [understanding – mother] through the *neshamah* [super soul] of the *neshamah* of the saint. It is associated with *Hokhmah*. The Tetragrammaton adding up to sixty-three then elevates the feminine waters through the *neshamah* of the saint. This is associated with

Binah. The Tetragrammaton adding up to forty-five then motivates the union between *Tiferet* [beauty – male] and *Malkhut* [kingship – female] through the *ruah* of the saint. The Tetragrammaton adding up to fifty-two then elevates the feminine waters through the *nefesh* of the saint. This is associated with *Malkhut* . . . In short, place the four letters of the Tetragrammaton before your eyes and meditate on them.

BANISHING OUTSIDE FORCES

In The Gate of the Holy Spirit, *Hayyim Vital depicted Isaac Luria's approach to banishing the outside forces.*

Meditate on the two names *Elohim Elohim* like this:

ALHYM ALHYM

Then intertwine the two names with the following vowels:

AeAe LeLe HeHe YeYe MaMa

Contemplate that each name *Elohim* has a numerical value of eighty-six, and hence the two names have a value of 172. Add to this an additional ten for the ten letters in both names, and you have 182, which is the numerical value of Jacob.

THE *YICHUD* FOR USING OTHER *YICHUDIM*

Hayyim Vital explained in The Gate of the Holy Spirit *that it is possible to use this* yichud *as a basis for making use of any other* yichudim.

This *yichud* is designated for a person who has meditated and has been worthy of experiencing his soul speaking to him. If he cannot actually express this communication with his lips, he should meditate with this *yichud* before any other *yichud* that he has used. This will allow him to bring his enlightenment from potential to action. Begin by meditating on the three expansions of the name *Ehyeh*:

ALF HY YOD HY   *yod* 161

ALF HA YOD HA   *aleph* 143

ALF HH YUD HH   *hey* 151

The first of these is expanded with *yods* and has a numerical value of 161. The second is expanded with *alephs* and has a numerical value of 143. The third is expanded with *heys* and has a numerical value of 151. Then meditate on the triangulation of *Ehyeh*.

AHYH	21
AHY	16
AH	6
A	1

Contemplate that this has a numerical value of forty-four. Add this to the 455 obtained earlier from the expansions and you have a total of 499. Now meditate on the name *Tzevaot* [Lord of Hosts]. This name is in *Yesod* [foundation], in its aspect as the Covenant of the Tongue. Contemplate that the numerical value of the name *Tzevaot* is also 499. After you complete this, you can make use of any *yichud* that you desire.

ELEVATION TO THE UNIVERSE OF *YETSIRAH*

For Luria it is possible to elevate one's nefesh *(soul) from* Asiyah *(making) to the Universe of* Yetsirah *(formation). As Hayyim Vital explained in* The Gate of the Holy Spirit:

Contemplate on the mystery of wings. Through wings man can fly and ascend on high. A bird cannot fly except with its wings. Paralleling the wings of a bird are the arms of man. These are five loves. These permeate the six directions of the body which parallel the six *sefirot*: *Hesed* [love], *Gevurah* [strength], *Tiferet* [beauty], *Netzah* [victory], *Hod* [splendour], and *Yesod* [foundation]. In the arms and the upper third of the torso these loves are concealed. In the lower parts of the body, they are revealed. It is for this reason that man flies with his arms that are his wings and not his legs or other limbs . . . Through these three names [*ABT YTH TZ, KRE SHTN, NGD YJHSH*] the loves that are in the arms and upper torso fly upwards to their root, which is *daat* [knowledge] of the *partzuf* [configuration] or *zer anpin* [small face (male)] for the purpose of union. Through this you will add strength to the loves. This will bring you to fly with greater strength, and you will be able to ascend from *Asiyah* to *Yetsirah*.

THE GOOD AND EVIL INCLINATIONS

In his Gate of the Holy Spirit *Hayyim Vital propounded his own theories about the mystery of creation and humankind's place in it. In his view, the soul is engendered by the* sefirot, *whereas his good impulse derive from the angelic realm. The soul and the* sefirot *constitv' person's essence and impel him to the good. However, his body and the evil impulse propel him towards evil. According to Vital, an individual's action has cosmic implications.*

The greatness of the soul has also been explained – it is a light engendered and drawn from the ten *sefirot* themselves without an intermediary . . . The nature of the good impulse and the evil impulse in human beings, in addition, has been clarified. They constitute two separate creations appended to man in addition to his soul. They comprise a light from the light of the angels, which is called 'the good creation', and a light from the light of the *kelippot*, called 'the evil creation'. The latter is external to the good impulse and serves as a shell around it. But the human soul itself is the most inward of all, and because it is inward it is also called 'the essence' of a person.

For this reason an individual has the freedom to incline in any direction he wishes for he is greater than them. His basic inclination is towards the good impulse since he is holy, as it is, and closer to it. But as for the body, its main inclination is towards the evil impulse, for both derive from the evil side and are also close to one another.

This is why there is a conflict between man's material self and the soul . . . It was necessary to create a man in whom should be included all creatures and all emanations, who was to link all worlds . . . to the very depth of the earth, for he would be the closest to receive the influences from the ten *sefirot*. Then by the perfection of his conduct he would transmit the abundance from the ten *sefirot* to himself, and from himself to the angels and then to the *kelippot*, in order that whatever would be sifted out from them should be perfected. Then this influence should be transmitted to the worlds themselves, 'vessels' and bodies of each different world. But if, God forbid, he should sin, he would damage all worlds.

DIVINE ILLUMINATION

In The Gate of the Holy Spirit *Hayyim Vital outlined the path whereby it is possible to receive divine illumination.*

ath . . . is the path followed by the saintly pietists of It demands that a person repent with great earnest- he has committed. Then he is to perfect his life by sitive commandments and by directing his prayer ighest purpose; by zealously studying the Torah for its own sake as an ox bows its head to the yoke until his strength is sapped; by confining himself to few pleasures, eating and drinking little; by rising at midnight or a little earlier; by turning away from all unbecoming traits; and by withdrawing from people, even from idle conversation. Then he should cleanse his body through continuous immersion. He should isolate himself for periods of time and contemplate the fear of God, continually putting the divine name *YHVH* before his eyes at all times, while making sure to empty his thoughts of the follies of this world. He is to be attached to God's love with great yearning. As a result of all this it is possible that he will merit illumination by the Holy Spirit.

A Vision of Preaching

In addition to Vital's presentation of Lurianic kabbalah, as well as his own mystical theories, he wrote his Book of Visions *while in Damascus. This work contains both his own dreams and visions and those of others.*

One Sabbath morning I was preaching to the congregation in Jerusalem. Rachel, the sister of Rabbi Judah Mishan, was present. She told me that during the whole of my sermon there was a pillar of fire above my head and Elijah of blessed memory was there at my right hand to support me, and then when I had finished they both departed.

A Synagogue Vision

In the Book of Visions *Hayyim Vital related another instance when Rachel had a vision while he was conducting the synagogue service.*

She saw a pillar of fire above my head when I conducted the *Musaf* [additional prayer] service in the Sicilian community on the Day of Atonement. This woman is accustomed to seeing visions, demons, spirits and angels, and she has been accurate in most of her statements from the time she was a little girl until now that she has grown to womanhood.

An Arab Vision

Hayyim Vital also related in the Book of Visions *that on one occasion he was visited by an Arab custodian of a mosque who claimed that he had seen him in a vision.*

He was a Jew-hater yet he kissed my hands and feet and entreated me to bless him and to write in my own handwriting whatever two or three words I would choose, so that he could hang them around his neck as a kind of amulet. I asked him why the sudden change of heart and he replied, 'I now know that you are a godly and holy man. For I am the custodian of a mosque. Last night at midnight I went out of the door of the mosque to relieve myself. The moon was shining so brightly at the time that it was as clear as noon. I raised my eyes and saw you flying through the air, floating for an hour above the mosque – you yourself, without any doubt.'

An Encounter with Moses Cordovero

Like those whom he quoted, Hayyim Vital was also subject to visionary experiences. In his Book of Visions he depicted his own dreams of special significance. In one case he encountered Moses Cordovero, who declared that he would pray for him in heaven.

I had a dream in which it was the day of the Rejoicing of the Law and I was praying in the synagogue of the Greeks in Safed. Rabbi Moses Cordovero was there, and another man greater than he in degree. When I awoke I forgot whether it was the *tanna* [sage] Rabbi Phinehas ben Jair of blessed memory or our contemporary, Rabbi Eleazar ben Yohai . . . After the prayers Rabbi Moses Cordovero said to me, 'Why do you torment yourself to such a degree to grasp the wisdom, with comprehension of the *Zohar* [*Book of Splendour*] that I, and all the sages of previous generations, have attained?' I replied, 'I shall continue to acquire as clear a comprehension as I can. If they do not wish it in heaven, what more can I do?' He said to me, 'If this is your desire to know the work to its very roots, more than the generations before you ever comprehended, I shall ascend to heaven to pray for you with all my might.'

The *Maggid* and the Divine Revelations

Born in Padua in the eighteenth century, Moses Hayyim Luzzatto studied the Bible, the Talmud, midrash, halakhic literature (legal sources) and classical languages, as well as other secular literature. In 1727, while immersed in kabbalistic speculation, he heard a voice he believed to be that of a maggid; subsequently he received further communications from this heavenly messenger, which he wrote down. In his teaching Luzzatto passed on these revelations to the members of a mystical circle. One of this group, Jekuthiel Gordon, described the activities of the group in a number of letters. In one addressed to Rabbi Mordecai Yoffe of Vienna, he discussed the role of this maggid.

There is here a holy man, my master and teacher, the holy lamp, the man of God, his honour Rabbi Moses Hayyim Luzzatto. For these past two and a half years a *maggid* has been revealed to him, a holy and tremendous angel who reveals wondrous mysteries to him. Even before he reached the age of fourteen he knew all the writings of the Ari [Isaac Luria] by heart. He is very modest, telling nothing of this event to his own father and obviously not to anyone else . . .

This is what happens. The angel speaks out of his mouth but we, like disciples, hear nothing. The angel begins to reveal to him great mysteries. Then my master orders Elijah to come to him and he comes to impart mysteries of his own. Sometimes Metatron, the great prince, also comes to him, as well as the Faithful Shepherd [Moses], the Patriarchs Abraham, Rabbi Hamnuna the Elder, and That Old Man and sometimes King Messiah and Adam . . . To sum up, nothing is hidden from him. At first permission was only granted to reveal to him the mysteries of the Torah but now all things are revealed to him.

The Transmission of Divine Mysteries

In a letter written to Rabbi Benjamin Ha-Kohen Vitale, Luzzatto explained and defended his mystical claims. Beginning with an explanation of his previous reticence to disclose the source of his kabbalistic teaching, Luzzatto declared that God had revealed these mysteries to him.

All the God-fearing come daily to me to hear the new things the Lord tells me. The young men who had previously walked in the ways of youth's vanities, now, thank God, have turned from the evil way to return unto the Lord . . . I have the obligation to encourage them until their feet have become firmly planted, as I hope, in the way of the Lord.

The Zohar and Tikkun

According to Luzzatto, the gates of divine grace were open when the Temple was in existence, but the 'Other Side' took over its power when it was destroyed. From that time events have occurred in accordance with the stages that require tikkun *(restoration). Pre-eminent among such* tikkunim *was the composition of the* Zohar. *Thus he continued in a letter to Rabbi Vitale:*

Rabbi Simeon bar Yohai was worthy of becoming the instrument by means of which this *tikkun* was performed, hence he composed the *Zohar*. However, the truth is that only a part of that illumination has emerged for the purpose of allowing Israel and the world as a whole to survive during the Exile. But for the real *tikkun* to be accomplished it is necessary for the thing to be permanent and unceasing so that divine grace is constantly renewed.

Tikkun and Personal Preparation

For Luzzatto every tikkun *depends for its efficacy on the preparation undertaken by the recipients. Concerning his own religious experience, Luzzatto explained in the same letter to Rabbi Vitale:*

At this time the Lord in his desire to be good to his people wished to reveal a new light in the category of the *Zohar*, which . . . is the illumination provided by the seminal drop. For this, in his mercy, he chose me. If you ask me about the state of my preparation, what can I say? The truth is that it is by the Lord's grace alone and has little to do with the state of my preparation for it. However, it is also true that I have been assiduous for years in carrying out *yichudim*. I perform a different *yichud* almost every quarter of an hour. The Creator now uses me as the instrument for the fulfilment of his purpose.

Heavenly Visitations

Continuing the account of his own revelations in this letter to Rabbi Vitale, Luzzatto described an experience that occurred when he was performing a certain yichud.

I fell into a trance. When I awoke, I heard a voice saying, 'I have descended in order to reveal the hidden secrets of the Holy King.' For a while I stood there trembling but then I took hold of myself. The voice did not cease from speaking; it imparted a particular secret to me. At the same time on the second day I saw to it that I was alone in the room and the voice came again to impart a further secret to me. One day he revealed to me that he was a *maggid* sent from heaven; he gave me certain *yichudim* that I was to perform in order for him to come to me. I never saw him but heard his voice speaking in my mouth . . . Then Elijah came and imparted his own secrets to me. And he said that Metatron, the great prince, will come to me. From that time onwards I came to recognize each of my visitations – souls whose identity I do know are revealed to me. I write down each day the new ideas each of them imparts to me.

4 Modern Mysticism
*c.*1750–present

Introduction

The early modern period witnessed growing dissatisfaction with
rabbinic leadership; as a consequence, a number of Jews sought to
achieve individual salvation through religious pietism. In this milieu
Israel ben Eleazer, known as the Baal Shem Tov (the Besht), advanced
a new approach to the tradition based on Lurianic *kabbalah* (mystical tradition). In his own writings he described his personal ascent
to the higher realms by performing the unification of the divine
name. In Jerusalem mystics at Bet El engaged in similar meditative
practices, which they believed enabled them to ascend to the heavenly heights – such a quest was based on a reinterpretation of Lurianic
kabbalah. Kabbalistic study was also encouraged by such rationalists
as the Vilna Gaon who, despite his criticism of the Hasidic movement, engaged in the study of the *Zohar* and the practical *kabbalah*.
Later in the century other kabbalists such as Alexander Susskind of
Grodno, as well as Hasidic masters, advocated various forms of
prayer-mysticism as a means of attaining divine illumination.
Following the tradition of these Hasidic writers, Kalonymus Kalman
Epstein of Cracow described his own experience and those of others.
Through worship, he explained, it is possible for the soul to ascend
the heavenly heights.

Among the leaders of Hasidism such figures as Dov Baer of
Mezhirich elaborated kabbalistic doctrines to explain how through
the breaking of the vessels, human beings can receive divine illumination. Such a view was further developed by Shneur Zalman of
Liady, the founder of *Habad* mysticism, who emphasized that
each individual is able to advance spiritually through study and

meditation. The system propounded by Shneur Zalman was redefined by his son and successor, Dov Baer of Lubavich, who put an
even greater stress on meditation. In the nineteenth century Aaron
Roth gathered together a small Hasidic community in Palestine
which adhered to a simple religious elevation. Finally, another
important mystical figure of the modern period, Abraham Isaac
Kook, reinterpreted kabbalistic concepts in an attempt to reconcile
Zionist aspirations with the coming of the Messiah.

THE BESHT

*According to tradition, the Baal Shem Tov (the Besht) was born in
Southern Poland; in the 1730s he travelled to Mezibozh where he performed various miracles and instructed his disciples about kabbalistic
love. By the 1740s he had attracted a considerable number of disciples
who passed on his teaching. In a letter to his brother-in-law, Rabbi
Abraham Gershon of Kutow, he gave a vivid account of his mystical
experiences.*

On the day of the New Year 5507 [1746] I engaged in an ascent of
the soul, as you know I do; I saw wondrous things in that vision that
I had never before seen since the day I had attained to maturity. That
which I saw and learned in my ascent it is impossible to describe or
to relate even from mouth to mouth. Yet as I returned to the lower
Garden of Eden I saw many souls, both of the living and of the dead,
those known to me and those unknown; they were more than could
be counted and they ran to and fro from world to world through the
path provided by that column known to the adepts in the hidden
science. They were all in such a rapture that the mouth would be
worn out if it attempted to describe it and the physical ear too indeli-
cate to hear it. Many of the wicked repented of their sins and were
pardoned, for it was a time of much grace . . . They also enjoyed
much rapture and ascended. All of them entreated me, to my embar-
rassment, saying, 'The Lord has given your honour great understanding to grasp these matters. Ascend together with us, therefore,
so as to help us and assist us.' Their rapture was so great that I
resolved to ascend together with them.

A VISION OF SAMAEL

*In the same letter to Rabbi Gershon, the Besht recounted that in a vision
he saw Samael act as an accuser. Filled with dread, he requested that
his teacher accompany him in his ascent.*

I went up step by step until I entered the palace of the Mes.
wherein the Messiah studies the Torah together with all the *tannai,*
(sages) and the saints and also with the seven shepherds. There I
witnessed great rejoicing and could not fathom the reason for it, so
I thought that, God forbid, the rejoicing was over my own departure
from the world. But I was afterwards informed that I was not yet to
die since they took great delight on high when through their Torah
I perform unifications here below.

IN STUDY AND PRAYER

*In his letter to Rabbi Gershon, the Besht gave advice as to the correct
procedure to follow when studying and praying.*

Whenever you offer prayers and whenever you study, have the intention of unifying a divine name in every word and with every utterance of your lips, for there are worlds, souls and divinity in every
letter. These ascend to become united one with the other and then
the letters are combined in order to form a word so that there is
complete unification with the divine. Allow your soul to become
embraced by them at each of the above stages. Thus all words become
united and they ascend so that immeasurable rapture and the greatest delight is experienced.

CLEAVING TO GOD

In his will the Besht argued that devekut *(cleaving to God) is of supreme
importance in the spiritual quest.*

It should be of indifference to him if he be considered as a person
of little knowledge or as one who is knowledgeable in the entire
Torah. The means for attaining this is *devekut*, cleaving to God, since
the preoccupation with *devekut* leaves one no time to think of such
matters, being constantly concerned with linking himself to the
realm on high, to God, praised be he. In whatever act he performs
in the service of God, he should consider that he thereby brings
delight to his Creator, praised be he, rather than for his own benefit ... A person should not think to himself that he is greater than
his neighbour because his service has reached the level of *devekut*,
for he is only like other creatures who were formed to serve God,
and God who endowed him with intelligence also endowed his
neighbour with intelligence.

BET EL

*f the eighteenth century a circle of those who during
listic meditation on the Godhead was established in
d in 1737 by Rabbi Gedaliah Hayon, these individu-
wn as the Mystics of Bet El. Later Rabbi Hayon was
succeeded by Shalom Sharabi, and his prayerbook contains the various
Lurianic meditations practised at Bet El. In an account of this group in
The Zohar in Moslem and Christian Spain, Ariel Bension, the son of
a member of Bet El, described their meditative practices.*

In Bet El joy was attained by no artificial means, but by silent meditation, by introspection in an atmosphere in which music blended
with men's thoughts, indeed a forgetfulness of externals. Each man's
eyes were turned inwards. Seeking to mine the wealth of his own
soul, he found there the soul of the universe. Amazed at his own
discovery of this hidden treasure the mystic pursues his course
upwards until he attains the ecstasy enthroned. In a silence in which
alone the soul may meet its God, destroyed worlds are reconstructed
and restored to the pristine perfection and this is the aim of the
kavvanot [intentions] – the meditation on the mystic meaning of
certain prayers with intention to bring restoration.

MEKHAVVENIM

The members of Bet El were known as mekhavvenim *(those who pray
with meditation). Unlike the Ashkenazic Hasidim, who were embroiled
in controversies with the* Mitnaggdim *(supporters of rabbinical
Judaism), Bet El welcomed both* Hasidim *and Rabbanites. As Ariel
Bension wrote in* The Zohar in Moslem and Christian Spain:

The *Hasidim* of Bet El did not look upon the Rabbinists as opponents
but rather as fellow seekers after Torah, and that union of groups
and sects, which had not been found possible elsewhere in Jewish
life, was accomplished at Bet El, where all were able to meet in
mutual respect and appreciation.

ECSTATIC FELLOWSHIP

*An expression of the fellowship of the members of Bet El was illustrated
by a document in* Siddur ha-Geonim ve-ha-Mekubbalim *signed by
Shalom Sharabi and others, in which the idea of unity was applied to
the group as a whole.*

We the undersigned, twelve of us, corresponding to the number of the tribes of Judah, agree to love one another with great love of soul and body, all for the purpose of giving satisfaction to our Creator through our single-minded association, although we are separated. Each man's soul will be bound to that of his associate, so that the twelve of us will be as one man greatly to be admired. Each one of us will think of his companion as if he were part of his limbs, with all his soul and with all his might, so that if, God forbid, any of us will suffer tribulation, all of us together and each separately will help him in every possible way . . . To sum up, from now and forever after we are met together, we are associated, we are joined, we are bound to the others as if we were one man.

Meditative Liturgy

As far as liturgy was concerned, melodies were added at Bet El to lengthen the period of meditation – they were sung aloud by the head of the pietists to stimulate and inspire mystical contemplation. In his account of Bet El in The Zohar in Moslem and Christian Spain, *Ariel Bension provided a description of the impact of such meditation on the listener.*

Hearing his voice rise in triumphant rapture to the words 'In love' – when the *mekhavven* must be prepared to die for the sanctity of the ineffable name 'In love' – the listener feels himself a heroic spirit ready to do battle for pure love. And he is able to understand the ecstasy of saints and martyrs as they joyfully gave themselves to the flames on a stake 'in love'.

Meditation on Lurianic *Kabbalah*

The mental activity of the mystics of Bet El was exemplified by their meditation on the details of the Lurianic system. Their liturgy in Siddur ha-Geonim ve-ha-Mekubbalim *contains a reflection on the thirteen qualities of mercy as found in Exodus 34:6–7.*

Know that the thirteen qualities mentioned in Micah: 'Who is a God like unto thee' . . . are the innermost influx of the Beard, which stem from the concealed Head of *Arikh Anpin* (Long Face). But the thirteen of the Torah portion *Ki Tissa* (When You Take), 'God merciful and gracious' . . . are the channels which bring the pure oil to the Beard. Know, too, that these thirteen perfections of the

Beard are divided into the *sefirot* [divine emanations] as follows. The first eight *tikkunim* [restorations] represent the eight *sefirot* and *Hokhmah* [wisdom], from the *tikkun* of *El* [God] the *Malkhut* [kingdom] of *Hokhmah*, down to 'keeping mercy', which is *Binah* [understanding] of *Hokhmah* (the order being in reverse). The last five *tikkunim* represent the *sefirot* of *Keter* [crown], from 'unto the thousandth generation', which is the *Hod* [splendour] of *Keter*, down to 'and clearing the guilty', which is the *Hesed* [love] of *Keter*. All this is in the category of surrounding lights and they are counted in reverse order. But with regard to the inner lights the opposite is the case – these are counted from above to below. This is the first *tikkun El*, which is the *Binah* of *Hokhmah*, down to 'keeping mercy', which is the *Malkhut* of *Hokhmah*. And so, too, with regard to the *sefirot* of *Keter*, they are counted from *Hesed* down to *Yesod* [foundation].

The Vilna Gaon

Born in Selets in the eighteenth century, Elijah ben Solomon Zalman, known as the Vilna Gaon, was the most important rabbinic scholar of his age. In addition to traditional rabbinic studies, he was adept at kabbalistic study. According to Hayyim of Volozhin in his Introduction to the Vilna Gaon's Commentary to the Sifra De-Zeninta, *he was unique in his learning.*

There are few only who can study the sources of our exoteric Torah . . . the Babylonian and Palestinian Talmud . . . let alone the innermost mysteries of the Torah . . . and the writings of the Ari [Isaac Luria] . . . For even the saintly disciples of the Ari could not penetrate the innermost depths of the meaning of this holy one of the most high, the Ari, except Rabbi Hayyim Vital . . . Until he, for his righteousness's sake, to magnify the law and make it honourable and to show us marvellous things from his law, made his merciful kindness exceedingly great over us; behold one like the son of man came with the clouds of heaven, to him glory was given, unique was this great man, none had been like him for a previous genera-tion . . . all the ways and paths of exoteric and esoteric wisdom were clear to him . . . this is the *gaon* [eminence] of the world, the *Hasid* [pious] and saint, our great and holy master . . . and with a mighty and marvellous adhesion to God, and a wonderful purity, until he was granted permission to penetrate the full understanding of things.

The Study of *Kabbalah*

According to Hayyim of Volozhin, it was an error to assume that the Vilna Gaon had a low opinion of kabbalah – rather mystical study was a central preoccupation.

While I am speaking of the great and marvellous holiness of the Torah of our great master, I am reminded of something that . . . makes my heart burn as a flaming fire . . . the rumours by ignorant and vain men in parts far away, who have never seen the light of his Torah and his saintliness . . . by saying that their holy *Zohar* was not found worthy in his eyes . . . let the lying lips be dumb that speak iniquity concerning the righteous . . . For their eyes can behold . . . this commentary on the *Zohar* . . . woe unto the ears that have to hear such slander, wherefore I found myself obliged faithfully to proclaim to the tribes of Israel his complete and mighty mastery of the whole *Zohar.*

Kabbalistic Study

Despite the Vilna Gaon's preoccupation with mysticism, he was unwilling to receive divine communications from maggidim, *as Hayyim of Volozhin explained:*

The most mighty and awesome of his virtues was this, that he did not allow himself to enjoy any good thing but that which he had laboured to acquire through wisdom and understanding . . . and with great effort. Wherever heaven had mercy upon him, and the fountains of wisdom, the most hidden mysteries were revealed to him, he regarded it as a gift of God and did not want it. Also when heaven wanted to deliver to him supreme mysteries without any labour or effort . . . through *maggidim*, masters of mysteries and princes of the Torah, he did not desire it . . . I heard from his holy mouth that many times *maggidim* from heaven appeared to him, requesting to deliver to him the mysteries of the Torah without any effort, but he would not listen to them.

Holy Mysteries

Instead of appealing to maggidim *for comprehension, the Vilna Gaon sought to gain knowledge of the Torah through study. In this way he believed God would grant him understanding. Nonetheless on various occasions Hayyim of Volozhin recounted that holy mysteries were revealed to him both in dreams and possibly also during waking moments.*

Holy mysteries were revealed to him by the Patriarch Jacob and by Elijah. In other places where he wrote in a general way that 'It had been revealed to him', I am not quite sure whether these were waking revelations or ascents of the soul to the celestial academy during his sleep. There can be no doubt that he certainly experienced ascents of the soul every night ... but concerning the revelations in his waking state I have nothing certain from him, for he kept these things secret ... However, from one amazing story which I heard from his holy mouth I inferred that he also had great revelations when awake.

PRAYER AND MARTYRDOM

Alexander Susskind was an eighteenth-century Lithuanian kabbalist who lived in seclusion in Grodno; his major work The Foundation and Root of Divine Worship *is a guide to the meaning and intention of prayer. For Susskind the purpose of meditation is to enable the worshipper to serve God and perform* tikkunim *in the higher realms. In a commentary on the verse 'Hear o Israel', he argues that such a type of worship takes place when a person is willing to sacrifice his life, and as a consequence God is exalted.*

As a result of this martyrdom, albeit only *in potentia*, in his thoughts, with great rapture and with the intention of sacrificing God's name throughout the worlds, the great name of our Maker and Creator, may he be exalted, is elevated and sanctified in all worlds, by both those on high and those here below.

THE RESOLVE TO FACE DEATH

In The Foundation and Root of Divine Worship, *Alexander Susskind reflected on the nature of a person's willingness to face death in order to honour God's name. In his view, such an intention does not mean anything until the believer makes a firm resolve that he will persevere even in the face of great danger.*

He should depict to himself that at this moment they are actually carrying out these forms of death and he should depict the pain and suffering that will be his ... the Creator ... who searches all hearts, sees his thoughts and the manner in which he depicts to himself the deaths and the tortures inflicted upon him and yet he survives the test. This is the real martyrdom even though it is only *in potentia*.

Types of Martyrdom

In Alexander Susskind's view, in The Foundation and Root of Divine Worship *it is obvious that every Jew will allow himself to be slain rather than be false to the Jewish faith. Such a soul will be willing to be slain in actuality rather than abandon the Jewish people. In contemplating these events the worshipper should depict to himself the nature of such martyrdom:*

When thinking of death by stoning, a man should imagine himself to be standing on the edge of a tower of great height and facing him are many belonging to the nations of the world and with an image in their hands, and they say to him, 'Bow to this image, otherwise we shall throw you off the edge of the tower.' He replies, 'I have no desire to bow to a graven or molten image, the work of men's hands, since our God is called the God of all the earth; he is the God of Israel. He is God in the heavens above and on the earth beneath; there is none else. To him will I bow the knee and prostrate myself.' He should then depict to himself that they cast him from the tower to the ground and he should also dwell on the terrible sufferings that will be his . . . He can, if he wishes, depict to himself another way of being stoned to death, namely, that they cast huge stones upon him.

Regarding death by burning, he should imagine that they want to compel him to bow to the image while they have a small pan filled with molten lead over a fire and they say to him, 'Unless you bow down to this image we shall pour this lead down your throat' . . . He should imagine how he opens his mouth of his own accord and how they pour the lead down his throat and the terrible sufferings he will endure. He can depict this form of death in another way, namely, that they cast him into a terrible fire.

The method of depicting death by decapitation is as follows – he should imagine that a sword is placed at his neck and he is told that unless he bows down to their image they will cut off his head . . . As for strangulation, he should imagine that they tell him that unless he bows to the image they will strangle him or drown him in a river.

RAISING HANDS IN PRAYER

Through mystical meditation, Alexander Susskind believed, the worshipper is able to perform mysteries related to the higher realms. Commenting on raising hands in prayer, he wrote in The Foundation and Root of Divine Worship:

When the fingers are spread out on high a man honours God with numerous supernal mysteries. He demonstrates the mystery of the ten *sefirot* as they are united and he blesses the Holy Name as it should be blessed. Moreover, he demonstrates the mystery of the unification of the inner chariots and the outer chariots so that the Holy Name is blessed on every side and all is united above and below ... Thus the whole side of the holy is elevated and all the 'Other Sides' are subdued so that they, too, acknowledge the Holy King.

RECITATION OF PSALM 29

Another example Alexander Susskind gave in The Foundation and Root of Divine Worship *of mystical meditation concerned the Sabbath evening service. Through the recital of 'Give unto the Lord' three times in Psalm 29, a special* tikkun *occurs on high; through the recital of 'voice' several times another* tikkun *is performed; and through the eighteen times the divine name is mentioned a special* tikkun *takes place. When reciting this psalm, the attitude of the believer should be as fervent in his devotion as one suffering martyrdom.*

When reciting the words, 'Give unto the Lord, O ye children of the mighty', a man should allow intense joy to enter his heart at the thought that we are called the children of the mighty, the children of Abraham, Isaac and Jacob ... When he recites, 'Give unto the Lord glory and strength. Give unto the Lord the glory due to his name,' he should take it upon himself to suffer martyrdom, depicting to himself some type of death he would suffer, and with all great rapture, for his martyrdom brings great glory to the Creator, blessed and exalted be he, and his great name becomes sanctified in all the worlds.

ZADDIKIM

According to critics of the Hasidim, *the concept of the zaddik (righteous person) is foreign to Judaism since there is no need for an intermedia-*

tory between God and human beings. In defen
attempted to explain the need for such figures in th
In a letter by the son of the eighteenth-century zad
of Lyzhansk, in No'am Elimelekh *the zaddikim*
to ascend the heavenly realms through the formul

For all that you see of the way the *zaddikim* serve the Lord in public is no more than a drop in the ocean compared with their inner life. In brief, they take care not to go outside their homes so as not to have to remain in an unclean place because of their holy thoughts. The writings of the Ari of blessed memory provide them with a key through which the fountains of wisdom are opened to them and great unifications [*yichudim*]. Even when they converse with other human beings their thoughts soar aloft towards the exaltedness of God, and they perform various unifications. When they study the holy *Gemara* [Talmud], fire actually consumes them, so great is their love and holiness. The fountains of wisdom, whether of the revealed or the secret things, are open to them.

HASIDIC PRAYER

In a letter written by Zechariah Mendel of Jaroslaw to his uncle in No'am Elimelekh *he defended himself against the charge that by joining the* Hasidim *he had forsaken the Jewish people. Extolling the deeds of the* zaddikim, *he emphasized that they occupy themselves with the Torah in devotion to God.*

There are among them such *zaddikim* as are capable of virtually raising the dead through the power of their prayer. I have seen it with my own eyes, not simply heard it by report, that on many occasions they brought to them invalids for whom there was no hope at all, yet through their pure prayer these were restored to perfect good health as before. In brief, they are hardly of this world at all but their thoughts are always in the worlds on high.

SELF-NULLIFICATION

Hasidic masters themselves defended their forms of prayer meditation. The eighteenth-century Hasidic rebbe *(spiritual leader), Nachman of Breslov, for example, taught a form of meditation in which the mystic concentrates on an external object such as a name or a mantra. According to Rabbi Nachman, such prayers should arise spontaneously. In his* Outpouring of the Soul *he wrote:*

must include yourself in God's unity, which is the imperative
existence. You cannot be worthy of this, however, unless you first
nullify yourself. It is impossible to nullify yourself, however, without
hithbodedut (mental self-seclusion) meditation.

When you meditate and express your spontaneous thoughts
before God, you can be worthy of nullifying all desires and all evil
traits. You will then be able to nullify your entire physical being and
become included in your root. The main time to meditate is at night.
This is a time when the world is free from mundane concerns. Since
people are involved in the mundane, by day, you will be held back
and confused so that you will not be able to attach yourself to God
and include yourself in him . . . it is also necessary that you meditate
in an isolated place . . . You must therefore be alone, at night, on an
isolated path, where people are not usually found. Go there and
meditate, cleansing your heart and mind of all worldly affairs. You
will then be worthy of a true aspect of self-nullification.

NOTHINGNESS

*In another work of this period the Hasidic mystic Rabbi Levi Yitzhak
Berdichov described in Aryeh Kaplan,* Meditation and Kabbalah *how
the mystic should concentrate on Nothingness – a form of meditation
which, he believed, enables one to ascend to the highest realm.*

When a person reaches the attribute of Nothingness, he realizes that
he himself is nothing since God grants him existence. He can then
declare that God 'creates' in the present tense. This means that God
is in the process of creating, even at this very moment.

When a person looks at himself and not at Nothingness, then he
has attained the level of 'somethingness'. He then can say that God
'created' – in the past tense. This means that God created him at an
earlier stage . . . We find in the writings of the Ari that the expression
'God is King' is an aspect of Nothingness. For when we declare that
God is King (in the present tense), this implies that he is currently
giving us existence. This is the aspect of Nothingness: we are nothing,
but God is giving us the power to exist. On the level of Nothingness,
everything extends beyond the laws of nature.

However, on the level of somethingness, all things are bound by
nature. The way in which we bind somethingness to Nothingness is
by means of the Torah and the commandments. This is the meaning
of the verse 'the Living Angels ran and returned' (Ezekiel 1:14), that
is from the level of Nothingness to that of somethingness. The *Zohar*

teaches that the commandments as well as the Torah are hidden and revealed. 'Hidden' alludes to Nothingness; 'revealed' applies to somethingness. They therefore bind something to Nothingness and Nothingness to somethingness . . . When a person wishes to bring new sustenance to all universes, he must attach himself to the dimension of Nothingness. This is the level in which all universes are not constricted. When a person nullifies himself completely and attaches his thoughts to Nothingness, a new sustenance flows to all universes . . . The individual in this way attaches the life force of all universes to Nothingness, which is on a higher plane than all worlds.

THE CONTEMPLATION OF DEATH

At the beginning of the nineteenth century Kalonymus Kalman Epstein, the leader of a Hasidic group in Cracow, was attacked for his enthusiasm in worship. In Maor va-Shemesh (The Light and the Sun), *he depicted his own ecstatic experiences as well as those of others. In his view, a person should contemplate the day of his death so as to attain a state of spiritual elevation.*

He should think of what will eventually take place and ponder his end – the separation of the hylic soul from the physical body. This is the end of all men, that the soul eventually becomes stripped of corporeality. Because of this, he should see to it now he is yet alive so that he can attain this state, namely the stripping away of the corporeality of this world from himself so that only the spiritual remains. Then he will become attached to the worlds on high and be saved from the evil inclination that causes him to sin.

HEAVENLY ASCENT THROUGH MEDITATION

According to Kalonymus Kalman Epstein, in Maor va-Shemesh *the true* zaddik *is able to proceed in his worship through all the upper worlds until he passes on to the* Ayn Sof. *When he reaches that state, he draws from there the influx of grace and blessing to the Jewish people.*

A person must study Torah, perform good deeds and offer supplications in order that he may be judged worthy of attaining to pure prayer. There are numerous accusers and antagonists on high who wish to hinder him in his ascent to the heavenly halls . . . Once he has ministered to the sages, studied Torah and offered up many supplications, he will be worthy of offering pure prayer. Then illumination will come to him from on high in order that he will truly be able to make petitions with a stripping away of corporeality. He will then progress in his contemplation until he reaches the place where comprehension is negated. Then he will know . . . that he has attained a high place, and subsequently through him will come the influx of grace to the community of Israel.

THE SECRETS OF THE TORAH

In another passage in Maor va-Shemesh *Kalonymus Kalman Epstein discussed the nature of the mystical state; in his view it cannot be explained to those who have never had such experiences. Discussing the nature of the secrets of the Torah, he wrote:*

It is necessary to understand the meaning of the secrets of the Torah. All Jews use this term, yet what does it refer to? It cannot denote the science of the *kabbalah* and the writings of the Ari of blessed memory and the holy *Zohar*, for a 'secret' is what cannot be communicated to others. However, the *kabbalah*, the writings of the Ari and the *Zohar* can be imparted to others and explained thoroughly to them. As a result these, having been revealed, are no longer secret. What then is the secret that is impossible to communicate? It is 'the secret of the Lord', that is to say, the essence of divinity that he was, is and will be and that he is the ground and root of all worlds.

ASCENT AND DESCENT

According to Kalonymus Kalman Epstein, in Maor va-Shemesh *only the* zaddikim *are able to penetrate the divine secrets. Through their heavenly ascent they can attach themselves to God before returning to the earthly realm.*

They occupy themselves deeply in the study of the Torah or in prayer with such great, burning enthusiasm that they experience the fragrance and sweetness of God, blessed be he. It would take very little for them to be annihilated, due to their great longing to become attached to God's divinity as they ascend from heavenly hall to heavenly hall and from spiritual world to spiritual world. They proceed in this way until they come to that high place where understanding is impossible except in the way one smells something fragrant, yet even then only in a negative sense, since what is there cannot be grasped by thought at all.

When they understand this, so great is their longing to attach themselves to the Divine, blessed be he, that they have no desire to return to the lowly world of the body. Yet since the one on high who caused the worlds to be emanated from himself wishes that the *zaddik* worship him in this world, he shows that person that the whole earth is full of his glory and that even in this world he is able to experience some of this sweetness and fragrance. As a result he is then willing to return.

TRANSMITTERS OF SPIRITUAL REFLECTION

In the view of Kalonymus Kalman Epstein, in Maor va-Shemesh *the* zaddikim *are unable to communicate their experiences to ordinary people. Instead translators of a lower spiritual rank must necessarily transmit such knowledge. These individuals play a major role in passing on knowledge of the heavenly realm.*

Each person can only comprehend this in proportion to his efforts and the refinement of his spiritual nature. The more a person understands of the Divine, the more he is able to attain profound degrees of comprehension through the refinement of his character. However, the more difficult it becomes for such an individual to explain and communicate to others the secrets of his heart, since he has so much more in his heart and has thoughts of what cannot be conveyed . . . However, the man who has not yet reached a profound comprehension of the being of God, blessed be he, such an individual can communicate to others what is in his heart since he has nothing there like the profundities of that other superior one [the *zaddik*]. From him ordinary folk are far more able to receive God's grace than from one who has attained great comprehension.

GOD'S PRESENCE

Among the leaders of the Hasidim, *the eighteenth-century scholar Dov Baer of Mezhirich played a central role in the development of later mystical thought. In his mystical writing Dov Baer formulated doctrines that furnished Hasidism with a speculative-mystical system. In his view God's presence is manifest in all things. Thus in his* Maggid Devarav le Yaakov (He Declares His Words to Jacob), *Dov Baer's disciple Shlomo of Lutsk recorded his theory.*

In every movement God is present since it is impossible to make any move or utter a word without the might of God. This is the meaning of the verse, 'The whole earth is full of his glory' [Isaiah 6.3] . . . There can be no thought except through the divine realm of thought. He is only like a *shofar* [ram's horn] that emits whatever sound is blown into it; if a person sounding it were to withdraw it would not bring forth any sound. Likewise, if God did not act in him he would not be able to speak or think.

REUNIFICATION

According to Dov Baer of Mezhirich, the divine emanation that is manifest throughout creation offers the basis for contact with God. The aim of human life is to reunite creation with the Creator. This is possible by focusing one's life and all worldly aspects on the divine dimension. This can be achieved by motivation that inspires action – all acts when motivated by the ultimate purpose of serving God become acts of unification. As Shlomo of Lutsk explained in Maggid Devarav le Yaakov (He Declares His Words to Jacob):

A person must not pray for his own concerns; rather he is to pray that the *Shekhinah* be redeemed from exile . . . even if one performs a *mitzvah* [commandment] but does not direct it for the sake of God, that is, he acts for some ulterior motive, he thereby brings about estrangement . . . For, as taught in the *Zohar,* the Torah and God are one, and if an individual performs a *mitzvah* properly, this *mitzvah* becomes one with God, one holy essence, constituted of one spiritual reality. On the other hand, if one performs it improperly he fashions an obstructing shell around the *mitzvah* so that it cannot unite itself with the holy essence of God.

ATTACHMENT TO GOD

For Dov Baer, the process of attachment to God brings about the unification of all the worlds below and the Divine. Thus Shlomo of Lutsk explained in Maggid Devarav le Yaakov.

When a person attaches himself to God, then all the worlds below him are united with God through him. In this way a person who is endowed with vitality through eating and wearing clothes, includes in himself the inanimate, vegetable, animal and rational life; they are all united with God through him.

THE ROLE OF ISRAEL

One of the most distinguished followers of Dov Baer of Mezhirich was Shneur Zalman, the founder of Habad *Hasidism. In his view regular study is a necessary spiritual exercise; from this standpoint he devel-*

oped the concept of the beinoni *(ordinary person). Unlike the* zaddik *who is an exceptional type, the* beinoni *is constrained by his own limitations. Nonetheless he is capable of striving towards perfection. Even though the* zaddik *is able to attain a higher level of spiritual elevation, he is not in fact of a higher rank than the* beinoni. *Thus he wrote concerning the role of the Jew in the* Tanya (It Has Been Taught):

The goal of creating man is that he might become submissive to God. This is to be explained as follows: the descent of the divine potency through many stages of self-limitation was to serve as a prelude to its return upwards in order to transform darkness into light. It is for this role that God created man on earth. Since this world is the lowly realm, covered with darkness, there is a need for many lights to illumine the darkness. God created man whose vocation is to serve as a light and a candle ... In this sense we should understand the call of Abraham to 'be a blessing' [Genesis 12.2]. He was to spread blessing throughout the world; it is similarly written of the children of Israel, 'They are a seed blessed by the Lord' [Isaiah 61.9] ... They were to spread influences from one world to another, from the world of concealment to the world of disclosure. In this fashion the divine realm would be disclosed. Those who bring about this disclosure are the Jewish people. They are the seed that discloses the Lord.

LEVELS OF PERFECTION

According to Shneur Zalman, it is possible for each individual Jew to attain a degree of perfection. As he explained in the Tanya:

The middle course is attainable by every individual; each person should try to reach it. A person who pursues the middle course does not despise the evil, which depends on the heart, and the times are not always conducive to such sentiments. But such a person is called on to depart from evil and do good through his behaviour, in deed, word and thought. Here a person can exercise freedom of choice and act, speak and think even in defiance of the heart's cravings ... a person should devote time to devise a strategy to condition himself to despise evil ... Thus it is with all the delights of this world. A wise individual sees that in the end they will rot and turn to worms and refuse. Therefore, let him delight in God, praised be he, by contemplating the greatness of the Eternal to the full extent of his capacities. Even though he recognizes that he will not reach this to its ultimate depth, but only by approximation, it is incumbent upon him to do what he can in fulfilment of the oath to be a *zaddik*.

LOVE OF GOD

In Iggeret ha-Kodesh (Letter of Holiness), *Shneur Zalman asserted that the soul's yearning to cleave to God grows out of love.*

The nearness of God is her [the soul's] good, and she desires it; it is painful for her to be separated from him by a barrier formed by worldly involvements. Such love is hidden in the heart of every Jew, even the wicked – this is the source of feelings of remorse. Yet because this love is hidden, in a kind of exile in the body, the *kelippah*, the evil power, can rule over it, and this is the folly that leads human beings to sin.

Man's service to God consists therefore in overcoming the evil power completely, banishing it from the body, from thought and speech and action. Then will he be able to release the prisoner from captivity so that this hidden love shall become manifest in all one's faculties, primarily in a person's mind and thoughts ... And the mind contemplates God, according to a person's intellectual capacity and the state of his culture, how he is the life of all life, and the life of his own soul in particular; he will naturally desire to cleave to him and be near him ... it is concerning this yearning, in active manifestation, the verse states, 'My soul yearns for God, for the living God' [Psalms 42.3].

ECSTASY

The system advanced by the Shneur Zalman was redefined by his son and successor Dov Baer of Lubavich, who placed an even greater emphasis on meditation. In the Tract on Ecstasy *Dov Baer sought to guide his disciples in the matter of contemplation leading to ecstasy. The majority, he believed, are incapable of attaining a state of ecstasy because they are absorbed with daily affairs. Even when these individuals are moved to ecstasy this state quickly disappears:*

We clearly observe among the majority of men, even among those who are well trained and well versed, desiring in truth the words of the living God, although they possess a talent for 'hearing', known as the 'hearing ear', yet it is really turned to dross, the very opposite. Such a person is moved to ecstasy when he hears and absorbs thoroughly in thought the details of a divine matter, exclaiming, 'Ha! I am warm, I have seen the light.' But here the matter ends. Even if he practises it two or three times, it is no more than a flash of a glance in mind and heart. It remains hidden and concealed in his soul, until it actually ceases to exit. Immediately he reverts to the interests of his body and does not tend it assiduously and constantly in order to fix it firmly in the soul with every kind of length, breadth and depth . . . All this is due solely to the malady of the natural soul. She has become accustomed to the materialism of the body. How then can she bear to receive the true sensation of the words of the living God?

MELANCHOLY

In Dov Baer of Lubavich's view, as expressed in his Tract on Ecstasy, *it is possible to overcome the disinclination to attain a permanent state of ecstasy by recognizing one's own spiritual inadequacy. From such a state of melancholy joy can spring forth.*

This I heard from my master and father of blessed memory, who himself heard it in these very words from the *Maggid* of Mezhirich, of blessed memory. A person is not capable of receiving the true secrets of the Torah and the deepest comprehension of the light of the *Ayn Sof*, to the extent that they become fixed truly in the soul unless he possesses natural melancholy . . . Then there will dwell within him the source of all life, the source of all to revive the spirit of the contrite . . . Then in everything he does in contemplating the secrets of the Torah, they will be delivered into his heart with true revelation as long as he has a humble heart. Similarly, regarding all the ways of divine worship, the Lord will accept him. Then his sighing and natural melancholy will be transformed into joy and delight because of the divine that rests upon his soul.

MARRIAGE AND STUDY

Born in 1806, the Hasid *Isaac Judah Jahiel Safrin described visions and revelations as well as his quest for the 'root' of individual souls in* Megillat Setarim (The Scroll of Secrets). *At the beginning of this work, he described his marriage and the progress of his study.*

At sixteen I married my true partner – she belonged to the *ruah* [spirit] aspect of my soul, yet since I had not reached the *ruah* aspect there were many obstructions to the match. However, due to the strength of my repentance and industry in study of the Torah, no stranger passed between us. Subsequently I attained many lofty stages in the holy spirit, the result of my industry in Tora study . . . my room was so cold since it had not been heated o⸍

during the whole of the winter. It was my custom to sleep only two hours a day, spending the rest of the time studying the Torah, the Talmud, Codes, the *Zohar*, the writings of our master [Isaac Luria], and the works of Rabbi Moses Cordovero.

DEMONIC FORCES

During his study, Isaac Safrin believed demonic forces attempted to persuade him to desist from such activity; in addition, he fell into a state of melancholy. During this time he consumed only a little water and bread and could derive no pleasure from study or prayer. The cold was so severe and the demonic forces so strong that he became totally confused. Nonetheless, in the midst of such despair he was over-whelmed by a sense of God's presence. As he explained in Megillat Setarim:

Suddenly during the day as I was studying the tractate *Yevamot* [Levrite marriages] in the name of the eternal God, in order to adorn the *Shekhinah* with all my might, a great light fell upon me. The entire house was filled with a marvellous light, the *Shekhinah* resting there. This was the first time that I had some taste of his light, may he be blessed. It was authentic, without error or confusion, a wondrous light and a most pleasant illumination beyond comprehension.

A VISION OF A VIRGIN

In Megillat Setarim *Isaac Safrin described a spiritual experience he had in the town of Dukla. When he went to the* Bet ha-Midrash *(the House of Study) to pray, he experienced the* Shekhinah *as a virgin surrounded by light.*

I wept in the presence of the Lord because of my anguish over the *Shekhinah*. In my distress I fainted and slept for a while. I saw a vision of light, a powerful radiance in the form of a virgin all adorned, from whom came a dazzling light. However, I was not worthy to see the face . . . her light was brighter than the sun at noonday.

OSHUA OF BRODY

sage in Megillat Setarim *Isaac Safrin described a dream* ad a vision of the Hasid *Joshua of Brody. Uncertain* dividual was alive in this world or the next, he asked d he come. 'From the world on high', he answered. Safrin *then asked how he fared in the heavenly domain. 'You fare well', the* Hasid *replied, 'And are of much worth there.' Isaac Safrin then asked:*

The previous week I was angry with my wife because she caused me great suffering. The result was that there departed from me the illuminations, souls and angels that accompany me.

'Did this cause any harm on high?' He did not reply so I embraced him and kissed him saying, 'Do not imagine that I ask these things because of my ambition to become a rabbi or Hasidic master. It is only that I long for my portion to be with the Lord God of Israel, among the people of Israel.' He replied, 'All is well.'

THE PROPHET ELIJAH

One Sabbath Isaac Safrin had a vision of Elijah who greeted him. Thus he wrote in Megillat Setarim*:*

I saw many souls who were critical of my book *Ozar ha-Hayyim* on the 613 commandments. They ordered me to stop writing any more and revealing such secrets. They showed me my book, complaining about many of the ideas in it ... they admitted that the teachings found in the book were true, but even so they came to the conclusion that I should not write any more. I replied that if the Lord would keep me in life I shall continue to write since we are commanded to know the reasons for the commandments. Afterwards I saw a spark of Elijah of blessed memory. I entreated him, 'Master, greet me I pray you!' He did so and I was filled with joy. I met many souls to whom I said, 'I have been working at being greeted by Elijah.' Then I awoke.

A VISION OF THE BESHT

In another passage of Megillat Setarim *Isaac Safrin related that he had a revelation of the Besht:*

I studied the Torah until midnight and finished the laws of Passover in the *Tur.* When I fell asleep I dreamed that I saw our master Elimelech of Lyzhansk who gave me an expression of great warmth. They told me that the place of the Master of the divine Baal Shem Tov was not too far from the place of the above-mentioned Master. Longing to see the face of our Holy Master I ran to his abode and stood in the outer room. They told me he was reciting his prayers in the inner sanctum; he opened the door and I saw the radiant form of our Master, the Baal Shem Tov . . . I was in such a state of joy and dread that I could not move, but he came up and greeted me with a smile on his face.

THE ASCENT OF A GOOD DEED

Born in 1894, Aaron Roth attended yeshivot *(rabbinical academies) in Galicia and Hungary, becoming an important Hasidic figure. At the end of his life he settled in Palestine where he established a small Hasidic community. His* Shomer Emunim *(The Guardian of Faith) contains a mystical tract 'Agitation of the Soul', in which he discussed the quest for divine illumination. In his view, such illumination takes place as a result of the unification that occurs in heaven due to a good deed's ascent. Heaven, he believed, is beyond time; thus, a good deed, Torah study, or prayer can ascend long after its actual performance. Quoting from* Pardes Rimonim, *a kabbalistic text by Moses Cordovero, he wrote:*

It follows that in proportion to the degree of engagement by a person in this world, so is the flow of divine grace to his *neshamah, ruah* or *nefesh*. It all depends on the amount of worship and the manner of its flaws, even if these had not taken place in his body. Occasionally it occurs that there is an influx to the soul when a person does a good deed or studies Torah. Then providence ordains that there will be an influx of soul so that it can become whole.

ESCAPE FROM DARKNESS

In Shomer Emunim *Aaron Roth argued that only a fool would wish to study Torah in its simple meaning and offer prayers in a similar spirit. Such a person would not believe in the possibility of new illuminations, but this understanding is mistaken since God affords illuminations to every generation that yearns for him. To explain this idea, Roth used a parable about a person locked in a dungeon.*

Near the dungeon is a huge precipice with a high wall. Beyond this wall are other walls, and beyond these there is a great and awesome place with many residences. Beyond all these is a house in which there shines a great and wonderful light, immeasurable and incomprehensible. This house is surrounded by many walls such that the hidden light can only shine through crevices and spaces . . . There are doors and windows through which light shines directly, and other windows through which it shines indirectly. It can occur that a certain door or window is opened so that the light shines directly on the person who dwells in darkness – he then experiences great joy, longing to escape from the dark dungeon so as to climb the precipice . . .

When a person is worthy of seeing this light his soul longs and is set on fire without limit until he feels he is about to expire in ecstasy. In his yearning he risks his life to open the door of his dungeon and springs energetically to experience the light. Yet as soon as he emerges the light is concealed, and he stands there at the foot of the precipice he is not capable of ascending because his limbs ache and the precipice is too steep and high.

A person at the top of the precipice then lowers a ladder to him. But it is very difficult to ascend by means of this ladder since agility is required as well as the willingness to risk one's neck by missing the step. He tries to ascend the ladder, but no sooner does he manage to climb a short way up than he falls back again. This takes place again and again until the Lord of the Manor has pity on him, and he reaches down to grasp his right hand so that he can pull him up.

Longing for Divine Illumination

Explaining the meaning of the parable about the dungeon, Aaron Roth stressed that two types of counsel are available to the people who long to escape from the realm of darkness. Thus he wrote in Shomer Emunim:

First they should cry out continually so that the Lord will take pity on them and cast a beam of light into their darkness. The second way is to long for the light and engage in contemplation on the greatness of the precipice and the awesomeness of the palace and the marvellous light within. This second approach is preferable since spirit calls out to spirit. Thus when a person's soul yearns to serve the Creator and when the Lord of the Manor observes his longing, that person can be spiritually elevated.

Spiritual Sleep

According to Aaron Roth, it is possible that a person can be so spiritually somnolent that he is unable to awaken to the divine light. This state is akin to a deep sleep or unconsciousness. Citing the writings of Rabbi Shalom Duber of Lubavich, Roth wrote in Shomer Emunim:

There is a sleep that is no more than a light nodding; this is when the sleeper is half-awake. There is the category of real sleep; there is the category of deep slumber; and there is the category of fainting, far worse, God forbid, where it is necessary to massage the sleeper, to strike him and revive him with every kind of medicine in order to restore his soul . . . And there is the category of still deeper unconsciousness that is known as a coma where, God forbid, only a tiny degree of life still remains in deep concealment . . . in this age we are in this deepest state of consciousness.

From Slumber to Divine Awakening

What can be done to draw human beings out of their slumber and return to an awareness of divine light? According to Aaron Roth in Shomer Emunim, *for some nothing can be achieved. Yet for others who are beginning to fall asleep, the best advice is to request that a friend awaken them. Such people should have mentors or friends who will converse with them about spiritual matters. In Roth's view, when Jews encourage one another in this way, God acts on their behalf.*

When holy Israelites meet together to encourage one another, the Holy One, blessed be he, gets there first . . . in order to harken to the holy words they speak . . . God gathers together all their words and records them in the book of remembrance. When there is an accusation against Israel . . . the Holy One, blessed be he, takes the book of remembrance and sees there those of his holy loves who long for the holiness of his name, blessed be he, and he is filled with joy . . . When the King rejoices, all sorrows and tribulations are automatically set at naught.

The Land of Israel

Born in Latvia in 1865, Abraham Isaac Kook received a traditional Jewish education, became a rabbi, and eventually served as Chief Rabbi of Palestine. In his mystical writings, Kook transformed religious messianic expectations into a basis for collaboration with modern Zionists. Life in the Diaspora, he believed, involves one in unholiness, whereas by settling in Palestine it is possible to live a spiritually unsullied life. Return to Zion is thus imperative for Jewish existence. As he wrote in 'The Land of Israel' in The Zionist Idea *edited by Arthur Hertzberg:*

A Jew cannot be as devoted and true to his own ideas, sentiments and imagination in the Diaspora as he can in *Eretz Israel*; outside it, they are mixed with dross and much impurity . . . In the Holy Land man's imagination is lucid and clear, clean and pure, capable of receiving the revelations of divine truth and of expressing in life the sublime meaning of the ideal of prophecy and to be illuminated by the radiance of the Holy Spirit. In gentile lands the imagination is dim, clouded with darkness and shadowed with unholiness, and it cannot serve as the vessel for the outpouring of the divine light.

Tikkun Olam

According to Abraham Kook, the redemption of Israel is part of a universal process involving all humans. The salvation of the Jewish nation is not simply an event of particular importance – it provides the basis for the restoration of the entire world (tikkun olam). Through the rebirth of the Jewish nation in their previous homeland, all humanity will be redeemed. As he wrote in 'The War' in The Zionist Idea *edited by Arthur Hertzberg, this is the universal meaning of the return to Zion.*

All civilizations of the world will be renewed by the renascence of our spirit. All quarrels will be resolved, and our revival will cause all life to be luminous with the joy of fresh birth. All religions will don new and precious raiment, casting off whatever is soiled, abominable and unclean; they will unite in imbibing of the dew of the holy lights, that were made ready for all mankind at the beginning of time in the well of Israel. The active power of Abraham's blessing to all the peoples of the world will become manifest and it will serve as the basis of our renewed creativity in *Eretz Israel*.

5 Contemporary Kabbalah 21st Century

Introduction

As we have seen the fundamentals of the medieval kabbalistic system were expanded by such luminaries as Moses Cordovero, Isaac Luria, the Baal Shem Tov, Nachman of Breslov, Levi Yitzhak Berdichov, Kalonymus Kalman Epstein, Dov Baer of Mezhirich, and Shneur Zalman. In the modern period interest in kabbalistic thought outside the Hasidic circle generally diminished with the exception of such figures as Yehuda Ashlag the author of *Sulam* (Ladder) who influenced the development of popular kabbalah; in recent years through his disciple Rav Berg the international Kabbalah Centre has today become the most influential proponent of kabbalistic thought worldwide.

Born in Warsaw in 1885, Ashlag was a descendent of scholars connected to the Hasidic courts of Prosov and Belz. In 1921 he moved to Palestine and worked as a labourer; later he was appointed rabbi of Givat Shaul, Jerusalem. In the 1930s he gathered around him a group of disciples who studied kabbalah and promoted the study of kabbalistic doctrine even for these who had not mastered rabbinic texts. In his view, knowledge of kabbalah can provide all persons with a taste of Godliness that would enable them to conquer their evil inclinations and advance spiritually.

During this period Ashlag published *The Talmud of the Ten Sephirot* which was a reworking of the thought of Isaac Luria; in addition he wrote an extensive commentary to this text. He also published *Sulam*, a translation and commentary on the *Zohar*. In this work Ashlag stressed the transformation of human consciousness from a state of desiring to receive, to desiring to give. Through the study of kabbalah, he believed, the mind opens to God's light, and the desire to give to others is developed. Ashlag believed that the coming of the Messiah meant that humans would give up their selfishness and devote themselves to loving each other.

Ashlag's main disciples included his sons Baruch Shalom and Shlomo Benyamin as well as Rabbi Yehuda Brandwein. Both Rabbi Baruch and Rabbi Brandwein influenced students who were involved in spreading Ashlag's interpretation of kabbalah. Brandwein's son-in-law. Rabbi Avraham Sheinberger, founded a commune in Israel, *Or Ganuz* (The Hidden Light) which combines Ashlag's communal ideas with a devotion to kabbalistic teaching.

In 1962 Rabbi Brandwein met Rav Philip Berg who had visited Israel from America. Trained in traditional *yeshivot*, Rav Berg was no longer a practising rabbi, but was deeply influenced by Rabbi Brandwein's teaching. In his autobiography, *Education of a Kabbalist*, Berg explains that he received the honour and responsibility of bringing the ancient wisdom of kabbalah to the world. As the devoted student of Brandwein, he established the Kabbalah Research Centre which today has 50 branches world-wide and has become the leading educational institution teaching the wisdom of kabbalah. Together with his sons Michael Berg and Yehuda Berg, Rav Berg has spread kabbalistic teaching to millions of adherents. In a wide range of publications the Bergs have spread Ashlagian kabbalism to disciples seeking for spiritual knowledge and insight.

Kabbalah for the Common Man

For Rabbi Brandwein, the message of kabbalah should not be exclusively for scholars. Rather, kabbalistic knowledge can enlighten every person. Quoting Rabbi Brandwein in Education of a Kabbalist, *Rav Berg emphasizes that kabbalah is for all people, not a chosen few:*

One night, during a break in our studies, I took the opportunity to ask Rabbi Brandwein a very basic question: 'Why are you concerned with the non-religious? Isn't it their business whether or not they choose to study and learn the ways of the Creator? As you yourself have commented on numerous occasions, we are not the spiritual policemen of the universe.' . . . He cleared his voice and sat comfortably in a chair . . . He began by discussing the war and destruction of the 20th century which in his opinion had caused the worst suffering and devastation of all time. From the development and use of nuclear weapons, to the Holocaust, to the bloody world wars and the many ethnic genocides, this was truly a century of pain, unparalleled in history in its darkness. While our masters of the past rested peacefully in the belief that the wisdom of kabbalah would be revealed to us in the end of days, this was no longer a belief we could comfortably share . . . We must make every effort to spread our knowledge amongst all peoples, so that every nation will worship The Creator and obey His laws and precepts. Only in this way can we hope to banish the darkness.'

Desire to Receive

In Education of a Kabbalist, *Rav Berg explains that he received Yehuda Ashlag's teachings from his teacher, Rabbi Brandwein. Studying Ashlag's* Sulam, *he learned the kabbalistic truth that God is Light and that it is the nature of human beings to desire to receive this light for them-selves alone.*

We are Vessels whose very essence is this Desire to Receive. If we receive the Light without meriting it, we feel pain and shame. By transforming our Desire to Receive for ourselves alone into a Desire to Receive for the Purpose of Sharing, we extinguish our pain, and ultimately become one with the Creator. Through study of the *Ten Luminous Emanations*, I become acquainted with these ideas. I can hardly convey how profoundly they moved me. To quote Rabbi Ashlag, 'One who studies the Talmud without grasping the secrets of the Torah and its mysteries is like one who sits in the dark without the Light of the Creator shining within him. Only through the wisdom of kabbalah can one grasp the ultimate purpose of Creation.'

Divine Light

Explaining Rabbi Brandwein's vision, Rav Berg asserts in Education of a Kabbalist *that the goal of human life is to bring the divine Light to the world.*

One day, Rabbi Brandwein took some time out from our busy schedule because he said he had something important to tell me . . . 'You must remember that it is the purpose of every truly spiritual person to bring the Light of the Blessed One to the world. This is the only way that darkness and negativity can be destroyed. Nothing else works. Expensive weapons, large armies, carefully planned wars –

they're all useless, and worse than useless. You must work very hard to fill yourself with Light, because only Light can wipe out the negativity of the world.'

Desire to Share

Of central importance in the kabbalistic system propounded by Rabbi Ashlag as explained by Rabbi Brandwein is the Desire to Share. This, he argued, should replace the Desire to Receive. In Education of a Kabbalist, *Rav Berg recounts Rabbi Brandwein's explanation.*

Rabbi Brandwein turned to me ... 'This is the cause of what I call "hatred for no reason", a disease which is horribly pronounced among certain individuals because of their great Desire to Receive. This gift which they have been given by The Creator, an unusually large spiritual vessel to contain His Light, is a mixed blessing; because it allows them to be filled with His Light, yet at the same time it can block them from true goodness. The larger the vessel is, the more a person might potentially have to give to others, yet, at the same time, the worse his hatred might be if he cannot transform his Desire to Receive into a Desire to Share. The challenge for such people is to transform their Desire to Receive into a Desire to Share. If this is not possible, however, the Desire to Receive will grow larger and larger until it swallows everything around it, and this unfortunately has been the case for humanity itself over thousands upon thousands of years. Human history is simply a record of self-serving desire run rampant, fuelled by hatred, envy, distrust. If someone has something we also have, we despise him.'

Spirituality and the Shattering of the Vessels

Drawing on Lurianic kabbalah, Rav Berg explains in Education of a Kabbalist *the significance of the shattering of the vessels in terms of spiritual growth. There is no coercion in spirituality, Rav Berg stated: if individuals are prepared to move forward spiritually, coercing them can actually be destructive.*

In kabbalah this idea is expressed through the primordial narrative often referred to as the Light and the Vessel. Before the Creation of the world, in fact, before the Creation of the universe itself, the love and beneficence of the Creator was the only reality. Kabbalah refers to this divine energy, love and beneficence as the Light. It is tempting to say that the Light was 'everywhere and at every moment,' though time and space as we know them had not yet come into being. In order to fully express its inherent nature to give and to share, the Light brought into being a receiving principle, the Vessel. As the Vessel received more and more Light, it gradually manifested a sharing intention of its own. Although it is an oversimplification to speak of these primal energies in human terms, one could say that the Vessel wanted to be more like the Light.

The Vessel therefore 'pushed back' the Light. It no longer wished to receive unearned benevolence. It desired to give and to share on its own. However, like an adolescent child who runs away from home and then quickly wants to come back again, the Vessel soon desired the return of the Light, despite the fact that it was no longer capable of allowing the Light in without internal conflict or pain. When the Light returned in full force, the Vessel simply shattered.

Science and Kabbalah

In Kabbalah for the Layman, *Rav Berg explains that there is a funda-mental distinction between kabbalah and science.*

Contemporary scientific thought and writing on the subject of the scientific method shows clearly that it is not the all – powerful tool that was once hoped. Perception, psychologists have finally realized, is an active process of sorting and interpreting, and not the passive, 'objective' absorption of stimuli implied by the scientific method. We must, in other words have a priori knowledge – a concept that comes very close to the idea of faith – before we can see and under-stand. In the kabbalah, there is no rigid distinction between physical and spiritual forms, and the picture presented is one of a total, unified, interrelated system . . . Science asks only how something exists within the dimensions or limitations of time, space, motion and causality; kabbalah goes further and confronts the question of why things exist at all.

The Absolute

According to Rav Berg, kabbalah provides the means whereby one can gain knowledge of the Absolute. As he explains in Kabbalah for the Layman.

Within the esoteric teachings of the kabbalah, we set foot on that road of the essence, the root, the point of view which alone can show us the straight and narrow path that leads to the Absolute. Once we can recognize the realm of the real, where the veils of the material word are stripped away, we may achieve universal oneness; having unveiled the mysteries and enigmas of life, we shall reach total truth.

God's Attributes

Explaining the central principles of kabbalah in Kabbalah for the Layman. *Rav Berg stresses we can know God through his attribute of sharing.*

Having said that God is complete and therefore good, we can now go on to describe the attribute through which we are aware of His existence – His desire to share. This is an extension of His goodness and is described in *Kabbalah as the Light.* Again we know that sharing, or imparting, is an attribute of goodness from our experience in this mundane world . . . This is the total of all we can know or say about God: that He is complete and lacks nothing, that He is good, that His attribute is the desire to impart, and that the manifestation of that desire is called positive energy.

The Process of Creation

For Rav Berg, the process of creation serves as the basis for understanding the desire to receive and the desire to share. In Kabbalah for the Layman, *he outlines the various stages.*

Since the desire to receive, which had been established in the en Sof, was now receiving the infinite beneficence of the Creator, there arose a feeling called 'Bread of Shame'. The vessel is receiving continuously, but can do nothing in return inasmuch as the Creator, being whole and lacking nothing, has no desire to receive. The vessel feels 'Bread of Shame' because it is unable to earn what it is receiving. Furthermore it is no longer merely a passive recipient as it was in the second state of the En Sof, before the appearance of the Desire to Receive. Now it actively wants the light that it lost in the third stage of Creation, but cannot take it due to its inability to offer anything in return; the metaphysical energy generated by this situation brings about the restriction, or *tsimsum*. It leads, by the principle of cause and effect, to a voluntary shutting-off of the Light, so that it can redress the existing lack of balance. The resultant emptiness and lack of light gives birth to the infinite desires to receive of the physical world, in which we are placed in an incomplete stage so that we can eliminate the 'Bread of Shame' by sharing with others who are also lacking, and in this way fulfil our own desires.

Ritual

In Kabbalah for the Layman, *Rav Berg explores the spiritual signifi-cance of the* mitzvot. *In his view, kabbalah can illuminate the spiritual significance of God's commandments.*

To place obedience at the pinnacle of the aims of the *mitzvot* and to interpret ritual and ceremonial observance of Torah as a revelation of dogmatic precepts leading to unquestioning subservience is to deny the spiritual origin of Divine commandments. It suffices merely to compare strict religious observance in the course of the last two hundred years with present adherence to Biblical law to realize the result of such an approach. Judaism is no longer spiritual and expe-riential but has developed into a rigid moral code, repellent to all but a small minority of the faithful. The teachings of kabbalah, in all their many forms, have yet to succeed in establishing once again the bridge linking the fundamental instincts of the individual Jew faced with the demands and strains of daily life with the quest for the inner meaning of the transcendent element of the celestial world.

The Study of Kabbalah

For Rav Berg, the study of kabbalah is not for the literal-minded: in order to penetrate the hidden mysteries of creation, there must be a conceptual leap by the seeker. In Kabbalah for the Layman, *he explains that the concepts of kabbalah are truths that transcend logic.*

Needless to say, then, the study of kabblalah is not for those who are extremely literal-minded. Rooted as they are in the illusion we call *Malkhut*, the so-called rationalist is incapable of making a concep-tual leap to the Divine word of Infinity from the limited language of Man. Logic cannot arrive at a conclusion that is beyond the realm of logic. Nor can the kabbalist's language be heard by those who do not know how to listen. Words, thoughts, and ideas amount to nothing unless their meanings are understood.

The language of kabbalah is of necessity a finite and therefore limited expression, but the concepts of kabbalah, the indelible truths, can be comprehended by those who read the *Language of the Branches* with their hearts and not just with their eyes, and who listen with their minds and not just their ears.

The Heart

A constant theme of Kabbalah for the Layman *is that the heart rather than the intellect is the source of true understanding. Here Rav Berg emphasizes that kabbalah can release us from illusion.*

Just as the principles of kabbalah cannot be perceived by the five common senses, neither can logic, reason, and common sense lead us to find the source of the river of our being. The Light cannot be learned, it must be experienced. Metaphysical connections cannot be made by means of the intellect – the tentacles of cosmic awareness proceed from the heart . . . The purpose of kabbalah is to remove the chains of logic and reason so that we may be released from the cage of our five common senses, for it is only by transcending the limits of these self-made linear boundaries that a direct link with the cosmic forces can be made. Only then can the real inner journey begin.

Reincarnation and Evil

In expounding the nature of kabbalah, Rav Berg stresses that the doctrine of reincarnation is a central doctrine. Why, he asks, is there human suffering if God is loving and good? The answer can be given in terms of rebirth of the soul. In Wheels of a Soul *he offers a solution based on kabbalistic teaching about reincarnation.*

The answer is, that the degree of evil and injustice abounding on this earth has nothing whatsoever to do with God. War, murder, violence, deceit and oppression are not the result of His will. Rather, they are the result of karmic debt and failing . . . souls laden with evil and in desperate need of correction before it is too late are flocking to this earth plane.

Recalling Past Lives

In Wheels of a Soul, *Rav Berg stresses that it is possible to recall past lives.*

To argue that, because there is no recall of past lives, past lives never existed is like contending that radio waves do not exist because they cannot be seen. Recall of past incarnations may not lie at our fingertips but they are there. All we have to do to reach them is to clean out the rust that has accumulated within our metaphysical computers. With memory restored, we can recall and understand past incarnations and thus clarify and explain the present one.

We have lost the ability to see things as they really are, and with that loss has gone the ability to become fully acquainted with our past lives. As a result, we plunge blindly through the present one using information gained in the past without the slightest awareness that we are applying it.

The Soul's Journey

Highlighting the concepts of desire to receive and desire to share, Rav Berg explains in Wheels of the Soul *that the improvement of the soul and its education is of fundamental importance yet its imprisonment in the body restricts its development.*

Only the soul provides the force which can integrate body energy into the whole and convert the whole to a 'Desire to Receive for the Sake of Imparting', and when that occurs, the soul has fulfilled its destiny by balancing its *tikune*. When that happens, the body dies. But in a truly righteous person body energy and soul energy become indistinguishable and disintegration of the body is no longer necessary . . . The soul view of the world is anchored in a Desire to Receive for the Sake of Sharing, and this view is translated as the goodness found in one quantity or another in almost all who breathe. The body, however, exists solely to receive for itself alone. It eats. It drinks. It hoards. It indulges its solitary vices and shares with no one. Even the inexorable gravitational pull of the earth upon which it walks feeds its desire, pulling the soul down, restricting and constraining it . . .

The Soul's Quest

In Rav Berg's view, the soul hungers for fulfilment. In Wheels of the Soul, *he explains that this is part of the divine plan. Yet, as when God created the vessels, so too the soul was faced with the same dilemma.*

Our souls were created for one reason only – the Creator, in whom all things are invested, had a Desire to Share. But, when the Creator existed alone, sharing could not occur. There were no vessels to hold the endless bounty pouring out of Him and so, with nothing more than desire, he created those vessels, which are our souls to this day, as the living Desire to Receive from His exalted light.

For time beyond our linear comprehension, our souls did just that. They received with no motive other than to receive for themselves alone. But as they were filled, a new yearning evolved – one that put them on a collision course with the Creator. Suddenly, in emulation of the Creator, our souls developed a Desire to Receive for the Purpose of Sharing. But they were faced with the same dilemma as that which faced the Creator Himself before He created his vessels. With every soul filled, there was no one and nothing with whom to share.

Thus – 'Bread of Shame.' Shame at receiving so much and giving nothing in return. Shame at being in a position in which the soul had no opportunity to say yes or no to the Creator and, by that exercise of will, prove itself worthy to receive and thus dispel the shame.

The shame led to rebellion – a mass rejection of the Creator's beneficence. When that happened, the light was withdrawn, darkness and the unclean worlds were created and all became finite – or limited – and thus in need of receiving. With those worlds came the clay bodies – vessels desiring only to receive for themselves alone – in which our souls reside. Here they forever struggle against body energy, to share.

Tikkune

The doctrine of reincarnation provides a framework for moral correction. In The Power of You, *Rav Berg emphasizes that in everything we do, we manifest aspects of ourselves from former lifetimes.*

Life for most of us represents a remake of a movie in which we previously acted, a reprise of tasks attempted earlier in which we somehow failed.

In the 21st century, humanity is merely living a motion picture rerun over and over again. Although human behaviour is genetically determined to a significant degree, the *Tikkune* directs and dictates our everyday thought patterns, feelings, and activities. Our behaviour, decisions, and reactions to our environments, as well as our most profound fears and moments of enjoyment, evolve directly from the results of accumulated lifetimes.

The law of *Tikkune* is really the law of fair play. By being permitted to sojourn in the physical world, the soul is given an opportunity to correct misdeeds performed in a previous lifetime. Unfortunately, it usually takes us far too many lifetimes to complete a *Tikkune*. Our lessons are patiently repeated day after day, year after year, and even lifetime after lifetime until the knowledge we have ignored comes crashing down on us, sometimes in a devastating fashion. And even then, many of us do not fully grasp the implications of that experience or make the necessary correction . . .

I am aware that these ideas challenge the conventional view of social scientists, who contend that it is culture and upbringing that shape human nature. Kabbalah teaches that every instant of our lives is fully determined by the cosmic forces prevailing at that time. Our actions are indeed controlled by the cosmos, but only to the extent that they were manifested in a prior lifetime. For example, if an individual committed crimes against humanity in a previous incarnation, his soul will return and will be faced with the same type of challenge he failed to meet in his past lifetime.

An Astrological Perspective

According to Rav Berg, astrology is linked to karmic correction. In The Power of You, *he affirms that the Tikkune process places an individual in an astrological position so that the stars will point us in the necessary direction.*

The various scenes of our past lifetimes always continue to exist as metaphysical channels of energy. When, in the present, we act in a negative manner that corresponds to negative behaviour in a past life, we become infused with negative energy intelligence. But this is not just malice on the part of the universe. Our prior negative activity is superimposed on our present life experiences in order to provide us with an opportunity to make a correction or *Tikkune*. Moreover, each day of our current lifetime corresponds to a particular movement in a former incarnation.

Despite the inviolability of the basic pattern of our destiny, we also have a degree of freedom that is almost without limitation. We can determine how the *Tikkune* process will take place within our present lifetime.

Astrology and Ethics

In The Star Connection, *Rav Berg emphasizes that knowledge of astrology can provide a framework for moral improvement.*

It is not my intent at this point to present a real case for the authenticity or validity of reincarnation. That ground already has been covered in *Wheels of a Soul*. The point is made here simply to emphasize that knowledge of astrology enables the individual to provide a rational explanation of life and its mysteries based on the ascertainable law of cause and effect. The metaphysical DNA is merely a printout of the individual's previous lifetimes. Based on his past behaviour, the infinite actions, both positive and negative, a new, reborn, metaphysical DNA is created as the embodiment of all these prior actions. The interface between the physical and metaphysical realm, between the present and composite metaphysical DNA, is the line-up of the astral bodies at the time of his birth.

The kabbalistic view of astrology, however, is dramatically different from the conventional pursuit of the science. Conventional astrology contends that the individual will take a course of action because of the arrangement of the stars, whereas kabbalah contends that the *Tikkune* process puts the individual in an astrological position so that the stars will impel him in the needed direction.

Spiritual Growth

In The Star Connection *Rav Berg stresses that spiritual growth is possible despite astrological influence.*

For all the inviolability of the basic destiny pattern, however, we have a degree of freedom almost without limitation to determine how the *Tikkune* process will be created in the present lifetime. The natal chart reveals the blinders and restrictions that will keep us from feeling free so that we ultimately can make use of the tools that are available by which we can transcend to another level of consciousness. Those blinders are of our own manufacture. We built them in prior lifetimes, but because we created them, we can break them and ascend to a higher level of consciousness . . . A commitment to self-knowledge and self-improvement is the first requirement of any individual who wishes to take control of his life and alter his destiny, but once that commitment is made, the results can be immediate and fulfilling. Not only will he be happier in the quest to elevate his soul, but he will find that pursuit of the goal begins to alleviate a great deal of the suffering initially dictated by his *Tikkune* pattern . . . Our present lifetime comprises the sum total of all previous lifetimes and only with comprehension of all previous experience can one find in his chart a composite of what he really has been. All that we have been, both good and bad, is contained in the present life chart.

Living in Light

The path to personal redemption is open to all individuals; their goal is to illuminate the world with divine light. In Taming Chaos, *Rav Berg stresses that such a motivation is linked to God's creative process.*

Upon creation we were imbued with the essence of the Creator. Because of our shame, what kabbalists call the Bread of Shame response to His beneficence, the Creator restricted His Light, as we must, in turn, restrict our desire to receive in order to free Him and flood the physical universe with His Light. Because we were created in His image, we are charged to do more than merely worship God. We are God, and we must act accordingly.

Meditation

For Rav Berg, the negative forces of the universe are controlled by the Opponent who thrives on chaos. He is the motivating force behind all human ills. Yet, as Berg illustrates in Taming Chaos, *he can be overcome. This can be achieved through a range of meditation techniques.*

Here are the tools such a person must muster if, having studied the Tree of Life sufficiently to understand the basics of its circuitry, she hopes to slip out of the Opponent's grasp and take control of her life. First, she must know precisely what it is she seeks from the beneficence of the Light. In this case, it is simply enough income to avert the present crisis. Then she needs the proper configuration of Hebrew letters, or one of the 72 names of God . . .

One does not need to be able to read, or even pronounce, the Hebrew words that will provide the software for activating meditation. Their power lies within the shape of the letters. One needs only to visualize them with intensity, to see them clearly even when the eyes are shut. With the basics assembled, we are now ready to embark. We are ready to make a minute alteration in consciousness that will allow us to depart from the fragmented noise and confusion of the Opponent and his Tree of Knowledge.

Kavanah

In Taming Chaos, *Rav Berg emphasizes that* kavanah *(intention) is of vital importance in mediation.*

Kabbalistic meditation techniques are more than just exercises. They employ a force called *kavanah*, without which there can be neither meditation nor prayer at any effective level. Like all Hebrew words, *kavanah* is tough to translate, emerging in various connotations as concentration, attention, intention, fervour, and devotion. But most of all, it stands for direction, and without the direction of *kavanah*, prayer and meditation are likely, at worst, to take practitioners nowhere in particular, or at best, to a location they really have no need or desire to reach.

Kavanah, then, is the driving force needed to keep a meditation on track and a prayer on target. In prayer, *kavanah* is the primary force, and the words of prayer are only of secondary importance. *Kavanah* is the soul of the prayer, and the meditative construct of light within light is the manifestation upon which the necessary intense concentration can be focused.

The 72 Names of God

Of primary importance in meditation, the 72 names of God are a set of powerful spiritual tools. According to earlier mystical sources they are found in three biblical verses in Exodus (Exodus 14:19–21) each of which contain 72 letters; these verses describe the miraculous parting of the Red Sea before the people of Israel, as they fled from the Egyptian army. In The 72 Names of God, *Yehuda Berg describes the power of these names.*

The energy that drives this ancient technology comes from these three verses and their 72 letters. The 72 Names of God are not 'names' in any ordinary sense. They have nothing in common with what you and I call ourselves. The 72 Names of God provide us with a vehicle to connect to the infinite spiritual current that flows through reality. God gave this cutting-edge technology to Moses to be shared with all people, so that humans could unleash their own God-like powers and attain control over the physical world.

Meditation and the 72 Names of God

As Yehuda Berg explains in The 72 Names of God, *the process of meditation is linked to the events at the Red Sea.*

First Verse

וַיִּסַּע מַלְאַךְ הָאֱלֹהִים הַהֹלֵךְ לִפְנֵי מַחֲנֵה יִשְׂרָאֵל וַיֵּלֶךְ מֵאַחֲרֵיהֶם
וַיִּסַּע עַמּוּד הֶעָנָן מִפְּנֵיהֶם וַיַּעֲמֹד מֵאַחֲרֵיהֶם:

God's angel had been traveling in front of the Israelite camp, but now
it moved and went behind them. The pillar of cloud thus moved from
in front of them and stood at their rear.

מ	מ	ע	א	שׁ	ל	א	ו	1
ד	פ	ע	ח	ר	פ	ל	י	2
מ	ג	מ	ר	א	ג	ה	ס	3
א	י	ו	י	ל	י	י	ע	4
ח	ה	ד	ה	ו	מ	ם	מ	5
ר	ם	ה	ם	י	ח	ה	ל	6
י	ו	ע	ו	ל	ג	ה	א	7
ה	י	ג	י	ר	ה	ל	ר	8
ם	ע	ן	ס	מ	י	ר	ה	9

Second Verse

וַיָּבֹא בֵּין מַחֲנֵה מִצְרַיִם וּבֵין מַחֲנֵה יִשְׂרָאֵל וַיְהִי הֶעָנָן וְהַחֹשֶׁךְ וַיָּאֶר
אֶת הַלָּיְלָה וְלֹא קָרַב זֶה אֶל זֶה כָּל הַלָּיְלָה:

It came between the Egyptian and the Israelite camps. There was
cloud and darkness that night, blocking out all visibility. All that night
[the Egyptians and Israelites] could not approach one another.

8	7	6	5	4	3	2	1
ה	כ	ל	ה	ל	י	ל	ה
ק	ר	ב	ז	ה	א	ל	ז
ה	ל	י	ל	ה	ו	ל	א
שׁ	ר	ו	י	א	ר	א	ת
י	ה	ע	ג	ן	ו	ה	ח
י	שׁ	ר	א	ל	ו	י	ה
ו	ב	י	ן	מ	ח	ג	ה
ח	ג	ה	מ	צ	ר	י	ס
ו	י	ב	א	כ	ב	י	מ

Now think about what has caused you to call upon this power at this
particular moment in your life. What Red Sea confronts you? What
army of Pharaoh is approaching from behind?

Do you see your present circumstance, however dire it may seem,
as an opportunity for revealing Light? . . . The Light will be revealed
through the power of the Names . . . It's best not to think of any

tcome you hope to realize. Instead, let your mind
wareness of the letters fills your consciousness. If
distracted by random thoughts, try to focus on
on the sequence of inhaling and exhaling – while
ue to rest on the letters. With each inhalation
.... power of the letters filling your body with Light. With
each exhalation allow the Light to enter you and permeate your
entire being.

After a few moments, close your eyes and visualize the letters
once more, but this time imagine them in white against a black
background. Let them occupy your mind as completely as possible.
Be aware that the letters are no longer on the page – they are within
you. They are your connection with a part of yourself that predates
your hopes and fears, and even your life. Through the letters you
can access the Light that is within you – the Light that comes from
the Creator.

The Evil Eye

*Within the kabbalistic system propounded by the Kabbalah Centre, the
concept of the Evil Eye is of particular importance. As Yehuda Berg
recounts in* The Red String Book, *the Evil Eye has a long history.*

Whatever you choose to call it, the concept of the Evil Eye goes back
thousands of years. The Evil Eye is mentioned in the Bible and is a
phenomenon acknowledged by Muslims, Jews and Christians. The
giants of Greek philosophy – Socrates, Plato and Aristotle – spoke
of it as well. Moses wrote about it. Kings, queens, and presidents
devised strategies to guard their nations against it.

The Red String

In The Red String Book, *Yehuda Berg explains that to protect oneself
from the effects of the Evil Eye, the kabbalists devised a spiritual technology: the Red String.*

The Red String allows you not only to remove negative influences,
but also to transform those influences into their spiritual opposite.
In this way, even the energy of the Evil Eye can change from a
channel for negativity into a profoundly healing form of energy . . .
After being wrapped around Rachel's tomb a prescribed number of
times, the Red String is cut into pieces and worn on the left

wrist . . . By wearing the Red String on your left wrist, you intercept, defuse, and convert any negative forces right at the front gate, their precise point of entry . . .

Just before putting on the string, you should ask for the strength and consciousness always to radiate compassion, kindness, and forgiveness toward everyone you meet, and always to feel a deep sense of appreciation for everything you have in your life, right now, so that you never have to cast a jealous eye toward another human being . . .

It is advisable to ask someone whom you trust, respect, and ideally, love – as well as someone with whom you have a 'connection' – to tie the Red String to your left wrist. First, have them tie the string closely around your wrist with a simple knot. Then have them repeat the gesture by knotting the string six more times for a total of seven knots. These seven knots signify white light (mercy) which contains the seven colours of the rainbow . . . As this person ties the string to your left wrist, he or she will say a prayer against the Evil Eye.

The Ana Becho'ach

According to Yehuda Berg, the Ana Becho'ach *is possibly the most powerful prayer in the entire universe. In* Dialing God, *he writes that it is a powerful technology that enables one to connect to the positive energy of each day and month; in addition it draws healing energy and protection.*

The *Ana Becho'ach* contains seven sentences, each sentence with six words. If we take the first letter of each word, we arrive at the 42-letter name ($7 \times 6 = 42$). Abraham the Patriarch, in his kabbalistic treatise, the *Sefer Yetzirah* (*The Book of Formation*), revealed the astrological secrets of the Aramaic letters and the signs of the zodiac. Second-century kabbalist Rav Nachumya ben Kakana was the first sage to reveal the 42-letter Name of God for our use.

The seven sentences of the *Ana Becho'ach* relate to the seven days of the week. Each day, we mediate upon the appropriate sentence to take control over that 24-hour period. Sunday connects to the first sentence. *Shabbat* (Saturday) connects to the last sentence. Each day, moreover, has its unique angel. We scan the letters to make up the angel's name before moving on to the next verse.

The power and energy of the *Ana Becho'ach* also enable us to connect to the planet and zodiac sign of each month of the year. Each month has its corresponding verse in the *Ana Becho'ach*.

In addition, kabbalistic technology teaches that the planets and the zodiac signs were created by Aramaic letters, so we also meditate upon the respective Aramaic letter that created both the planet and the zodiac sign of that particular month.

❶ חסד, יום ראשון   Sunday, Chesed   אבג יתץ

אָנָּא בְּכֹחַ. גְּדוּלַת יְמִינְךָ. תַּתִּיר צְרוּרָה:

ana   vecho'ach   g'dulat   yeminecha   tatir   tzerurah

Meditation: Power of redemption. Unconditional love. Removing the negative influence of physical matter from our lives. Tapping into the Tree of Life reality. Remembering yesterday's lessons.

❷ גבורה, יום שני   Monday, Gvurah   קרע שׂטן

קַבֵּל רִנַּת. עַמְּךָ שַׂגְּבֵנוּ. טַהֲרֵנוּ נוֹרָא:

kabel   rinat   amecha   sagvenu   taharenu   nora

Meditation: Closing the gates to the Satan. Forgetting all limited and limiting thoughts. Destroying negative influences at the seed level, thus preventing bad things from happening in the first place. Overcoming our reactive nature. Transforming chaos to miracles and wonders.

Further Reading

Abelson, J. 1969. *Jewish Mysticism.* Brooklyn, NY, Sepher-Hermon Press.

Ariel, D. 1992. *The Mystic Quest: An Introduction to Jewish Mysticism.* New York, Pantheon Books.

Baile, D. and S. Gershom 1978. *Kabbalah and Counter-History.* Cambridge, MA, Harvard University Press.

Band, A.J. 1978. *Nahman of Bratslav, the Tales.* Mahwah, NJ, Paulist Press.

Ben-Amos, D. and J.R. Mintz 1994. *In Praise of the Baal Shem Tov.* Northvale, NJ, Jason Aronson.

Berg, Michael, 2001. *The Way.* New York, John Wiley and Sons.

Blumenthal, D.R. 1978, 1983. *Understanding Jewish Mysticism: A Source Reader,* vols 1 and 2. Hoboken, NJ, Ktav Publishing House.

Bokser, B.Z. 1994. *From the World of the Cabbalah.* Northvale, NJ, Jason Aronson.

—— 1993, *The Jewish Mystical Tradition.* Northvale NJ, Jason Aronson.

—— trans. 1978. *Abraham Isaac Kook.* Mahwah, NJ, Paulist Press.

Buber, M. 1991. *Tales of the Hasidim.* New York, Pantheon Books.

—— 1988. *Hasidism and Modern Man.* Atlantic Highlands, JN, Humanities Press Interational.

—— 1988. *The Tales of Rabbi Nachman.* Atlantic Highlands, NJ, Humanities Press, International.

—— 1960. *The Origin and Meaning of Hasidism.* New York, Horizon Press.

Chanan, M.D. 1983. *The Zohar.* Mahwah., NJ, Paulist Press.

Dan, J. 1987. *Gershom Scholem and the Mystical Dimension of Jewish History.* New York, New York University Press.

Dresner, S. 1994. *The Zaddik.* Northvale, NJ, Jason Aronson.

Epstein, P. 2001, *Kabbalah.* Boston, Shambhala.

Fine, L., trans. 1984. *Safed Spirituality: Rules of Mystical Piety, the Beginning of Wisdom.* Mahwah, NJ, Paulist Press.

Gottlieb, E. 1976. *Studies in Kabbalistic Literature.* Tel Aviv, Tel Aviv University.

Green, A. 1992. *Tormented Master: A Life and Spiritual Quest of Rabbi Nahman of Bratslav.* Woodstock, VT, Jewish Lights Publishing.

Halevi, Z'ev ben Shimon. 2000. *Astrology and Kabbalah.* London: The Urania Trust.

Halperin, D.J. 1980. *The Merkabah in Rabbinic Literature.* New Haven, CT, American Oriental Society.

Idel, M. 1988. *Kabbalah: New Perspectives*. New Haven, CT, Yale University Press.

Jacobs, L. 1981. *The Palm Tree of Deborah by Moses Cordovero*. Brooklyn, NY, Sepher-Hermon Press.

—— 1977. *Jewish Mystical Testimonies*. New York, Schocken Books.

—— 1972. *Hasidic Prayer*. Washington, DC, B'nai B'rith Book Service.

——trans. 1963. *Tract on Ecstasy* by Dov Baer of Lubavich. London, Vallentine, Mitchell and Co.

Kalisch, I. 1978. *The Sepher Yezirah*. Berkeley Heights, NJ, Heptangle Books.

Kaplan, A. 1995. *Meditation and Kabbalah*. Northvale, NJ, Jason Aronson.

Katz, S.T., ed. 1978. *Mysticism and Philosophical Analysis*. Oxford, Oxford University Press.

Kramer, S.G. 1966. *God and Man in the Sefer Hasidim*. New York, Bloch Publishing Co.

Langer, J. 1993. *Nine Gates to the Chasidic Mysteries*. Northvale, NJ, Jason Aronson.

Levin, M. 1975. *Classic Hassidic Tales*. New York, Viking Penguin.

Newman, L.I. 1987. *The Hasidic Anthology*. Northvale, NJ, Jason Aronson.

Parrinder, G. 1995. *Mysticism in the World's Religions*. Oxford, Oneworld.

Rabinowicz, H.M. 1970. *The World of Hassidism*. London, Vallentine, Mitchell and Co.

Schaya, L. 1973. *The Universal Meaning of the Kabbalah*. trans. Nanch Pearson. New York, Viking Penguin.

Scholem, G.G. 1995. *Major Trends in Jewish Mysticism*. New York, Schocken Books.

—— 1995. *The Messianic Idea in Judaism*. New York, Schocken Books.

—— 1995. *Zohar: The Book of Splendour*. New York, Schocken Books.

—— 1990. *Origins of the Kabbalah*. trans. Allan Arkush. Princeton, NJ, Princeton University Press.

—— 1978. *Kabbalah*. New York NAL Dutton.

—— 1969. *On the Kabbalah and Its Symbolism*. New York, Schocken Books.

—— 1960. *Jewish Gnosticism, Merkavah Mysticism and Talmudic Tradition*. Hoboken, NJ, Ktav Publishing House.

Seltzer, R.M. 1982. *Jewish People, Jewish Thought*. New York, Macmillan.

Singer, S.A. 1971. *Medieval Jewish Mysticism Book of the Pious*. Northbrook, Ontario, Whitehall.

Tishby, I. 1991. *The Wisdom of the Zohar: Anthology of Texts*, vols. 1 to 3. Oxford, Oxford University Press.

Waite, A.E. 1976. *The Holy Kabballah*. New York, Carol Publishing Group.

Weiner, H. 1992. *Nine and One Half-Mystics: The Kabbala Today*. New York, Macmillan.

Werblowsky, R.J.Z. 1977. *Karo: Lawyer and Mystic*. Philadelphia, Jewish Publication Society.

References

The Apocryphal Wisdom of Solomon, in J. Abelson, *Jewish Mysticism*.

Apokalypse des Pseudo-Propheten und Pseudo-Messias.

Abraham Abulafia, A. Jellinek, in *Graetz-Jubelschrift*, 1887.

Ben Porat Josef, 1992.

Berit Menuhah (The Covenant of Rest), Warsaw, 1883.

Dialing God, Yehuda Berg, New York: The Kabbalah Centre, 2004.

Education of a Kabbalist, Rav Berg, New York: The Kabbalah Centre, 2000.

Etz Hayyim (The Tree of Life), Jerusalem, 1960–3.

Even ha-Shoham (The Onyx Stone), Jerusalem MS 8″ 416.

Gate of Kavvanah, Jewish Theological Society, MS 1822:9, p. 43a,b.

Ginat Egoz (The Nut Garden).

Hebrew Scriptures, RSV, Oxford: Oxford University Press, 1971.

Hekhalot Rabbati (The Greater Chambers), In S.A. Wertheimer, *Batei Midrashot*, vol. 1, Jerusalem, 1968.

Iggeret ha-Kodesh (Letter of Holiness), Shklov, 1814.

Introduction to Lamentations Rabba, S. Buber, 1899.

Introduction to the Commentary on Sifra De-Zeniuta, Vilna, 1820.

Kabbalah for the Layman, Vols 1–2, Rav Berg, New York, Kabbalah Press, 1981, 1988.

Kidushat Levi, Bereshit (Holiness of Levi, Genesis), Jerusalem, 1958.

Likkutei Biurim, Warsaw, 1868.

Likutey Moharan (Anthology of Our Master, Rabbi Nahman), Ostroy, 1806.

Maggid Debarav le Yaakov (He Declared His Words to Jacob), Lvov, *c.* 1697.

Maggid Mesharim (Teller of Upright Words), Amsterdam, 1704.

Maor va-Shemesh (The Light and the Sun), Breslau, 1842, Tel Aviv, 1965.

Megillat Setarim (The Scroll of Secrets), published by N. Ben-Menahem, 1944.

Meirat Eyanyim (Light of the Eyes), Oxford MS 1619; Munich MS 14; Jerusalem, 1979.

Midrash Bereshit Rabba, Jerusalem: Wahrmann, 1965.

Mishnah, P. Blackman, Judaica Press, vols. 1 to 7, 1951–6.

Noam Elimelekh, Lvov, 1787.

Or Ha-Sekhal (Light of the Intellect), Vatican Ms. 233; Munich Ms. 92; Jerusalem Ms. 8″ 3009.

Or Neerav (Pleasant Light), Venice, 1587.

Pardes Rimonim (The Orchard of Pomegranates), Cracow, 1592.

Philo, Loeb Classical Library Series, vols 1 to 10, 1929–62.

Philosophie und Kabbalah, A. Jellinek, Leipzig, 1854.

Rabbi Moshe Hayyim Luzzatto u-Venei Doro, published by S. Ginzburg, 1937.

Re'iyyot Yehezkiel (Vision of Ezekiel), in Temirin, *Mosad ha-Rav Kook*, 1, 1972.

The Secret of Secrets, in *Sefer Raziel*.

Sefer ha-Bahir (Book of Bahir), ed. R. Margaliot, 1951.

Sefer ha-Hezyonot (Book of Visions), Jerusalem, 1954.

Sefer ha-Ot (The Book of the Sign), in *Apokalypse des Pseudo-Propheten*.

Sefer Hasidim (Book of the Pious), Jerusalem, 1957; Frankfurt am Main, 1924.

Sefer Hayyei ha-Olam ha-Ba (Book of the Life of the World to Come), Jerusalem, 8" 540.

Sefer Raziel (Book of Raziel), Medzibezh, 1818.

Sefer Yetsirah (Book of Creation), York Beach, ME: Samuel Weiser, 1990.

Shaar ha-Kavvanot (The Gate of Intentions), Tel Aviv, 1962.

Shaar Ruah Hakodesh (The Gate of the Holy Spirit), Jerusalem, 1962.

Shaarei Orah (The Gates of Light), Jerusalem, 1970.

Shaarei Tzedek (The Gates of Justice), Leiden MS (Arner 24,2).

She'elot u-Teshuvot min ha-Shamayyim (Responsa from Heaven), ed. R. Margaliot, 1975.

Shomer Emunim (The Guardian of Faith), 1964.

Shulhan Arukh Shel Ari (The Set Table of Isaac Luria), Jerusalem, 1961.

Talmud, Shulzbach, 1756–63.

Taming Chaos, Rav Berg, New York, Kabbalah Publishing, 2003.

Tanya (It Has Been Taught), Shklov, 1806.

The 72 Names of God, Yehuda Berg, New York, The Kabbalah Centre, 2004.

The Power of You, Rav Berg, New York, The Kabbalah Centre, 2004.

The Red String Book, Yehuda Berg, New York, The Kabbalah Centre, 2004.

The Star Connection, Rav Berg, New York, The Kabbalah Centre, 1986.

Wheels of a Soul, Rav Berg, New York, The Kabbalah Learning Centre, 1995.

Yesod Ve-Shoresh ha-Avodah (The Foundation and Root of Divine Worship).

The Zionist Idea, ed. A. Hertzberg, New York: Athenaeum, 1959.

Zohar, Jerusalem, 1953.

The Zohar in Moslem and Christian Spain, 1932.

Index